11+ English

For GL Assessment – ages 10-11

Revising for GL 11+ English can seem overwhelming... but don't panic! This CGP book is overflowing with vital practice to sharpen your skills.

Every topic is explained with revision notes, tips and examples, and there are heaps of questions to help make sure all that knowledge has sunk in.

What's more, there are mixed practice tests and two full practice papers, plus answers to every question at the back — it really is the complete package.

How to access your free Online Edition

This book includes a free Online Edition to read on your PC, Mac or tablet.
You'll just need to go to **cgpbooks.co.uk/extras** and enter this code:

4052 0194 0497 7451

By the way, this code only works for one person. If somebody else has used this book before you, they might have already claimed the Online Edition.

Complete
Revision & Practice

Everything you need to pass the test!

Contents

About the 11+

What's in the 11+ 1
What's in the 11+ English Test 2
How to Prepare for the 11+ 3

Section One — Grammar

Nouns and Pronouns 4
Verbs 7
Adjectives, Adverbs and Prepositions 10
Determiners 12
Sentences, Clauses and Phrases 14
Conjunctions 18
Standard English and Formal Writing 20
Answering Grammar Questions 22
Practice Questions 26

Section Two — Punctuation

Starting and Ending Sentences 30
Commas, Dashes and Brackets 33
Apostrophes and Hyphens 36
Speech 38
Colons and Semicolons 40
Answering Punctuation Questions 42
Practice Questions 44

Section Three — Spelling

Plurals 48
Homophones and Homographs 50
Prefixes and Suffixes 52
Silent Letters and Double Letters 54
Other Awkward Spellings 56
Answering Spelling Questions 58
Practice Questions 60

Section Four — Writer's Techniques

Alliteration and Onomatopoeia 64
Imagery 66
Abbreviations 69
Irony and Rhetorical Questions 70
Idioms, Clichés and Proverbs 72
Synonyms and Antonyms 74
Answering Word Type Questions 76
Practice Questions 78

Section Five — Comprehension

Reading the Text 82
Understanding the Questions 84
Answering Comprehension Questions 86
Practice Questions 88

Section Six — Writing

How to Prepare for the Writing Test 90
Make a Plan 92
Write in Paragraphs 94
Make It Interesting 96
Writing Practice 99
Practice Questions 100

Mixed Practice Tests 102
Practice Paper 1 114
Practice Paper 2 126

Glossary 138
Answers 140
Index 156

Published by CGP

Editors:
Keith Blackhall, Claire Boulter, Izzy Bowen, Tom Carney, Eleanor Claringbold,
Holly Robinson, Matt Topping and Rebecca Russell.

With thanks to Emma Crighton and Robbie Driscoll for the proofreading.

With thanks to Lottie Edwards for the copyright research.

Every effort has been made to locate copyright holders and obtain permission to reproduce sources. For those sources where it has been difficult to trace the originator of the work, we would be grateful for information. If any copyright holder would like us to make an amendment to the acknowledgements, please notify us and we will gladly update the book at the next reprint. Thank you.

ISBN: 978 1 78908 599 0

Printed by Elanders Ltd, Newcastle upon Tyne.
Clipart from Corel®

Based on the classic CGP style created by Richard Parsons.

Text, design, layout and original illustrations © Coordination Group Publications Ltd. (CGP) 2020
All rights reserved.

Photocopying more than one section of this book is not permitted, even if you have a CLA licence.
Extra copies are available from CGP with next day delivery • 0800 1712 712 • www.cgpbooks.co.uk

About the 11+

What's in the 11+

Make sure you've got your head around the basics of the 11+ before you begin.

The 11+ is an Admissions Test

1) The 11+ is a test used by some schools to help with their selection process.
2) You'll usually take it when you're in Year 6, at some point during the autumn term.
3) Schools use the results to decide who to accept. They might also use other things to help make up their mind, like information about where you live.

If you're unsure, ask your parents to check when you'll be taking your 11+ tests.

Some Schools test a Mixture of Subjects

1) Depending on the school, the 11+ might test different subjects.
2) There are four main subjects that can be tested in the 11+, so you might sit papers on some or all of these:

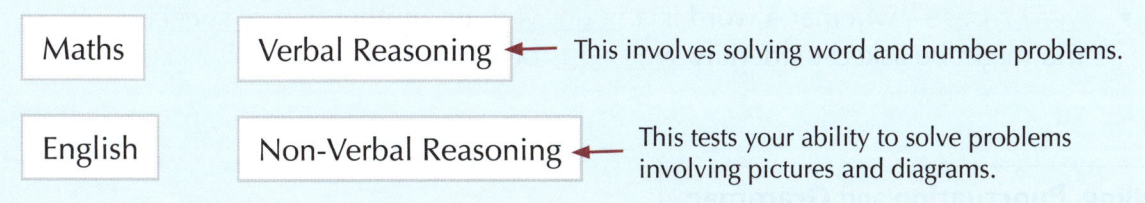

Maths
Verbal Reasoning ← This involves solving word and number problems.
English
Non-Verbal Reasoning ← This tests your ability to solve problems involving pictures and diagrams.

3) This book will help you with the English part of the test.

Get to Know what Kind of Paper you're taking

Your paper will either be multiple-choice or standard answer.

Look out for the tips at the end of each topic — they'll give you practical advice about the test, plus revision tips and extra hints to help you crack 11+ English.

Multiple-Choice

1) For each question, you'll be given some options for the answer.
2) On the separate answer sheet, you'll need to mark your answer with a clear pencil line in the box next to the option that you think is correct.

Standard Answer

1) You'll be expected to write down the correct answer for some questions, but you may have some options to choose from for others.
2) You'll usually mark or write your answer on the question paper.

Check which type of question paper you'll be taking, so you know what it looks like and where your answers go. Try to do some practice tests in the same format as the test you'll be taking, so you know what to expect on the day.

What's in the 11+ English Test

Get your brain ready for 11+ English by reading about the different question types.

11+ English will test your **Reading** and **Word Knowledge**

1) You'll already have picked up loads of the skills you need for the test at school.
2) There are three main types of questions that can crop up:

Comprehension

The text could be fiction, non-fiction or a poem.

You'll be given one long text or several short texts to read. You'll have to answer questions which test how well you understand the text. The questions might ask you about:
- what the text means — what happens in the text, what a character is like or how they feel, or what the writer's purpose is.
- word meanings — what some of the trickier words in the text mean.
- word types — whether a word is a noun, verb or another part of speech. You might be asked to identify synonyms or antonyms.

Spelling, Punctuation and Grammar

- You'll have to find spelling and punctuation mistakes in a short text, or add punctuation marks to sentences.
- For grammar questions, you'll usually need to choose the best word from a list of options to fill gaps in a text so that it makes sense.

Writing

Some tests include a writing task. You'll get a title or topic and you'll have between 20 minutes and an hour to write a short story or essay. You might have to continue the extract used in the comprehension part of the test. You'll need to:
- write in standard English (that means no slang or text speak).
- make sure your writing is structured with a beginning, a middle and an end.
- use plenty of techniques to make your writing interesting.

3) Some tests include shorter tasks that test your word knowledge. You might have to find the odd one out from a list of words, make compound words, reorder words to make a sentence, or reorder sentences to make a story.
4) You need to have a good vocabulary and to understand how words and sentences are made.

About the 11+

How to Prepare for the 11+

Give yourself a head start with your English preparation — be organised and plan ahead.

Divide your Preparation into Stages

1) Find a way to prepare for the 11+ that suits you. This may depend on how much time you have before the test. Here's a good way to plan your English revision:

> Use this book to revise strategies for answering different question types. Read through the study notes and follow the worked examples carefully — make sure you understand the method used at each step.
>
> ↓
>
> Do plenty of practice questions, concentrating on the question types you find tricky.
>
> ↓
>
> Sit some practice papers to prepare you for the real test. We've included two papers at the back of this book to get you started.

2) When you first start answering 11+ English questions, try to answer the questions without making any mistakes, rather than working quickly.
3) Once you feel confident about the questions, then you can build up your speed.
4) You can do this by asking an adult to time you as you answer a set of questions, or by seeing how many questions you can answer in a certain amount of time, e.g. 5 minutes. You can then try to beat your time or score.
5) As you get closer to the test day, work on getting a balance between speed and accuracy — that's what you're aiming for when you sit the real test.

There are Many Ways to Practise the Skills you Need

The best way to tackle 11+ English is to do lots of revision and practice. This isn't the only thing that will help though — there are other things you can do to hone the skills you need for the test:

1) Read a lot, and make sure you read a mix of fiction and non-fiction writing.
2) If you're reading an article in a newspaper or magazine, underline the key facts as you read — picking out the most important information from a text is a really useful skill.
3) If you come across any unfamiliar words, look them up in a dictionary. Keep a vocabulary list to make sure you remember new words.
4) Play word games or do crosswords to build up your vocabulary.
5) Write stories, letters to friends and relatives or articles to go with news headlines that you find interesting. You could also keep a diary to practise your writing skills.

Section One — Grammar

Nouns and Pronouns

Revising nouns and pronouns should feel pretty familiar — you use them all the time.

A Noun is the Name Given to Something

There are three types of noun that you need to know about:

1) Proper Nouns are Names

1) Proper nouns are the names of particular people, places or things.
2) They always start with a capital letter.

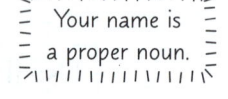
Your name is a proper noun.

Heather is going to Rome. 'Heather' and 'Rome' are proper nouns.

Let's go to Froggatt's Foods on Thursday. 'Froggatt's Foods' and 'Thursday' are also proper nouns.

2) Common Nouns are Things

1) Common nouns are names for people or things in general. They don't usually start with a capital letter.
2) Here are some examples:

Eat your banana at the table.

That man is carrying a suitcase.

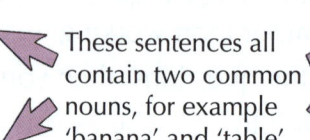
These sentences all contain two common nouns, for example 'banana' and 'table'.

The monkey sat in a tree.

Pour some water into my cup.

3) Some common nouns can also be abstract nouns. Abstract nouns are things you can't see, hear, touch, smell or taste, like emotions or ideas. Here are some examples:

loyalty	sadness	pride
truth	anger	hope
happiness	courage	despair
fear	friendship	jealousy

3) Collective Nouns are for Groups of Things

1) Collective nouns name a group of things.
2) They don't start with a capital letter either.

Remember, a collective noun isn't the same as a plural noun.

A bunch of flowers   A herd of cows   A troop of monkeys

'bunch', 'herd' and 'troop' are all collective nouns.

Section One — Grammar

Nouns and Pronouns

A **Pronoun** can be used **Instead** of a noun

1) Pronouns are words that you use instead of nouns.
2) They save you from repeating the same noun again and again.

Ralph took his dog for a walk but it ran away from him. ← 'it' and 'him' are pronouns — they replace the nouns.

These **Pronouns** are all **Important**

1) 'I', 'you', 'he', 'she', 'it', 'we' and 'they' are used when a person or thing is doing an action. → She won't remember, but I will.
2) When the person or thing is having the action done to it, you need 'me', 'you', 'him', 'her', 'it', 'us' or 'them'. → Neha told him to take care of them.

Some pronouns show **Ownership**

Possessive pronouns tell you who owns something.

| mine | yours | his | hers | ours | theirs |

The paperclips in the corner are mine. ← This tells you who the paperclips belong to.

There is also a type of pronoun called a relative pronoun. See p.15 for more on these.

You may be asked to **Recognise** different types of **Nouns**

EXAMPLE: Circle seven common nouns in the passage below.

> The incompetent wizard became nervous when Emma asked him for a demonstration. "OK," he said, "I'm going to turn your hair orange." He closed his eyes and muttered the spell. The crowd of people gasped — Emma had been turned into a frog.

Method — Pick out the types of things and people

1) Work through the passage one sentence at a time.
2) Be careful not to circle proper or collective nouns.

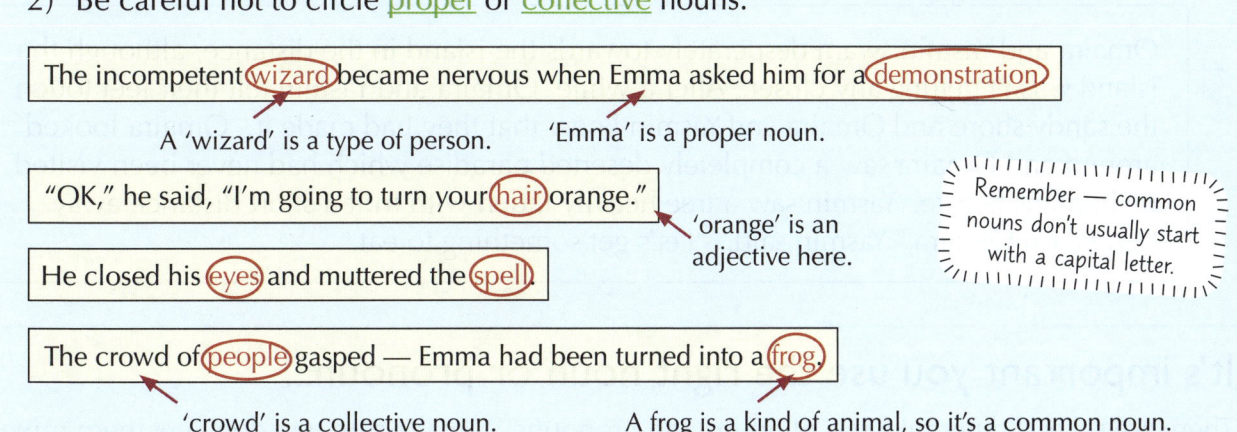

The incompetent (wizard) became nervous when Emma asked him for a (demonstration).
A 'wizard' is a type of person.   'Emma' is a proper noun.

"OK," he said, "I'm going to turn your (hair) orange."
'orange' is an adjective here.

He closed his (eyes) and muttered the (spell).

The crowd of (people) gasped — Emma had been turned into a (frog).
'crowd' is a collective noun.   A frog is a kind of animal, so it's a common noun.

Remember — common nouns don't usually start with a capital letter.

Section One — Grammar

Nouns and Pronouns

> Make sure that you can **Replace a Noun** with a **Pronoun**

 Rewrite the passage below, replacing nouns with pronouns where needed.

> PC Wade is investigating a robbery at Mr Forde's house last Tuesday. PC Wade knows that the robber was female, but nobody has provided any leads about the robber. The robber stole a valuable vase and Mr Forde is offering a £1000 reward for the valuable vase when it is returned.

Method — Look for nouns that are repeated

1) Work through the passage <u>one sentence</u> at a time.
2) Look for places in the passage where the <u>same noun</u> is <u>repeated</u>.
3) Make sure that the sentence <u>still makes sense</u> when you replace the noun.

> PC Wade is investigating a robbery at Mr Forde's house last Tuesday.

This sentence is fine. There are no repeated nouns.

> PC Wade knows that the robber was female, but nobody has provided any leads about her.

You can't replace 'PC Wade' with 'he' here — it wouldn't be clear if the pronoun referred to PC Wade or Mr Forde.

'The robber' is repeated here. The robber is female, so change the second 'the robber' to 'her'.

> She stole a valuable vase and Mr Forde is offering a £1000 reward for it when it is returned.

'The robber' can be replaced by 'she' here to avoid repetition.

'Valuable vase' is repeated in this sentence. You can add 'it' here instead.

Practice Questions

1) Write down whether these words are proper nouns, common nouns or collective nouns.

   a) <u>swarm</u> of bees   d) cauliflower   g) <u>class</u> of children
   b) December   e) lady   h) hockey
   c) Scotland   f) ostrich   i) Sue Shaw

2) Rewrite the passage below, replacing nouns with pronouns where they are needed.

> Omaira and Yasmin swam desperately towards the island in the distance, although the island wasn't getting any closer. After a while, Omaira and Yasmin felt their feet touch the sandy shore and Omaira and Yasmin knew that they had made it. Omaira looked around and Omaira saw a completely deserted paradise which had never been visited by humans before. Yasmin saw a tree heavily laden with fruit a short distance away. "Come on Omaira," Yasmin said. "Let's get something to eat."

It's important you use the right noun or pronoun...

There are several different types of nouns and pronouns — make sure you don't get them mixed up.

Section One — Grammar

Verbs

In the sentence 'I adore treacle tart', the verb is 'adore'.

A Verb is a Doing or Being Word

1) Verbs are <u>action</u> words — they show what a person or thing is <u>doing</u> or <u>being</u>.

   | Carl sings in the shower. | ← The verb is 'sings'. | Shirley is happy. | ← The verb is 'is'. |

   Every sentence has to have a verb.

2) The verb needs to <u>agree</u> with the <u>subject</u> of the sentence (the person or thing doing the action). If they don't agree, the sentence <u>won't make sense</u>.

Verbs tell you When something is Happening

1) The <u>tense of a verb</u> can indicate whether something is happening in the <u>past</u> or <u>present</u>.

   | Roberta played the lead role. | ← past tense → | Roberta has played the lead role. |

   | Roberta plays the lead role. | ← present tense → | Roberta is playing the lead role. |

2) You can also use verbs to talk about things that <u>will happen</u> in the <u>future</u>.

   | Roberta will play the lead role. | | Roberta will be playing the lead role. |

   Sometimes there's more than one verb together in a sentence.

Active and Passive Verbs tell you Who or What

Active Verbs tell you Who's Doing the Action

1) <u>Active verbs</u> make it clear <u>who's</u> doing the action.
2) The sentence is about the person or thing doing the action. The verb agrees with the <u>person</u> or <u>thing</u> that does the action (the subject).

   | Tricia opened the parcel. | | We think fighting is wrong. |

   This noun is the subject.   This is the verb.   This pronoun is the subject.   This is the verb.

   Most verbs in sentences are active verbs.

Passive Verbs tell you What's Being Done

1) <u>Passive verbs</u> say <u>what's happening</u>, but they <u>don't</u> always say <u>who</u> is doing the action.
2) Passive sentences <u>focus</u> on the <u>action</u>. You can add in the person or thing doing the action using '<u>by</u>', but you don't have to include it.

   | The parcel was opened by Tayo. | | It is agreed that fighting is wrong. |

   The sentence tells you who opened the parcel.   This sentence doesn't tell you who agreed that fighting is wrong.

   A verb is made passive with the correct part of 'to be', e.g. 'was', 'is', 'are' etc.

Section One — Grammar

Verbs

Some verbs can show you how **Likely** something is

1) Words like '<u>would</u>', '<u>could</u>' and '<u>can</u>' are modal verbs.
They usually come with <u>another verb</u> in the sentence.

| I can join you afterwards. |

In this sentence, 'can' is the modal verb.
There's also <u>another</u> verb — 'join'.

2) <u>Modal verbs</u> can show how likely an action is.
3) Some modal verbs show something is <u>less</u> likely.

| He might come with us. | | You could fall over. | | I may bring my sister. |

4) Others can show something is <u>more</u> likely.

| Lara will find the keys. | | She must be worried about the test. | | We shall leave at 9 am. |

You might be asked to **Identify** modal verbs

Circle the verbs in the passage below that tell you how likely something is.

> Piet glanced at his watch and darted into the station. He could still catch his train if he was quick. However, he would need to find the right platform. "I must get this train," he said to himself. "I will be late to the concert if I have to wait for the next one."

Method — Look for verbs that describe possibility

1) Work through the passage <u>one sentence</u> at a time.
2) Look for places where verbs tell you <u>how likely</u> something is.

| Piet glanced at his watch and darted into the station. | ← There are no modal verbs in the first sentence.

| He (could) still catch his train if he was quick. |

'could' is a modal verb because it shows how likely it is that Piet will catch his train.

'was' doesn't tell you how likely the action is — it's not a modal verb.

| However, he (would) need to find the right platform. |

This is another verb that describes how likely an action is.

| "I (must) get this train," he said to himself. |

'must' comes next to another verb ('get'), which helps you to work out that it's a modal verb.

| "I (will) be late to the concert if I have to wait for the next one." |

'will' is a modal verb — it tells you Piet is very likely to be late.

Section One — Grammar

Verbs

Make sure that you can Use Verbs in the Correct Tense

In each sentence, one verb has been used incorrectly.
Rewrite the sentences using the correct form of the verb.

a) "Quick, everyone went to your lookouts!" ordered the firefighter.
b) The ball was kick into the back of the net.
c) My rabbit is escape at this very moment.
d) Yesterday, my brother refuse to clean his bedroom.

Method — Work out when the action is happening

a) "Quick, everyone go to your lookouts!" ordered the firefighter. — The firefighter is issuing an instruction in the present tense. So, 'went' needs to change to 'go'.

b) The ball was kicked into the back of the net. — The clue here is 'was' — it tells you that the sentence is in the past tense. So, 'kick' needs changing to 'kicked'.

c) My rabbit is escaping at this very moment. — 'is' tells you that this sentence is in the present tense and it's still happening. So, 'escape' should be 'escaping'.

d) Yesterday, my brother refused to clean his bedroom. — 'Yesterday' tells you that the sentence is in the past tense. So, use 'refused' instead of 'refuse'.

Practice Questions

1) Underline the verb in each sentence.
   a) The concert starts in ten minutes' time.
   b) We finished our fun run in record time, despite the bird costumes.
   c) Clotilde perfected the decorations on the birthday cake.
   d) I love rock-climbing in the Lake District during the summer.
   e) Christmas brings increased business to many toy shops.
   f) The steam train rushes past on its way to the coast.

2) Circle the correct verb to complete each sentence.
   a) Barney has *eating / eat / eaten* all of my popcorn.
   b) I have *going / been / went* to South Africa on holiday.
   c) Hannah's knee is *hurted / hurts / hurting* after she fell over.
   d) You should *are / have / go* home or you'll be late.
   e) What time do you think you will *arriving / arrive / arrived*?
   f) The dolphin is about to *leaps / leaping / leap* out of the water.

TEST TIP — **Use the whole sentence to choose the correct verb...**
Use clues in the rest of the sentence to find the right answer. Look at the words around the verb to help you work out the tense of the sentence and who is doing the action.

Section One — Grammar

Adjectives, Adverbs and Prepositions

There are a few terms coming up for you to get your head around. First up is adjectives...

Adjectives are Describing Words

Adjectives describe Nouns

Adjectives tell you more about nouns.

Luke was wearing a green jumper.

This describes the jumper.

The monster was huge and scary.

These adjectives describe the monster.

Some adjectives Compare People or Objects

Comparatives are for comparing one thing with another thing.

Sarah is taller than Noelani.   Elizabeth is less cheerful than Philip.

Superlatives tell you which is the most, least, best or worst of a group of things or people.

Yours is the biggest house on the street.   Brett is the richest person I know.

Adverbs describe Verbs

Adverbs often end in -ly.

1) Adverbs tell you how, when, where or why an action is done.

The choir sings beautifully.   The girls played football yesterday.

This adverb tells you how they sing.   This adverb tells you when they played football.

2) Adverbs can also describe adjectives or other adverbs.

Tracy is quite happy.   The theatre is totally full.   He walked very slowly.

3) Some adverbs, like 'maybe', 'perhaps' and 'probably', show how likely something is.

I will probably see you tomorrow.

Prepositions tell you the Relationship between Nouns or Pronouns

1) Prepositions are words like 'under', 'in front of', 'between' and 'with'.
They tell you how things are related in terms of location or space.

Dennis sat under the bridge.   Jessica climbed into the car.

2) Prepositions can also tell you when things are or why they happen.

Make sure you get there before 7 pm.   I can't play because of my broken leg.

Section One — Grammar

Adjectives, Adverbs and Prepositions

You might have to **Identify Parts of Speech**

   Circle the adverbs in the passage below.

> With millions of tourists each year, Paris is easily one of the most popular cities on Earth. Two of the attractions that are hugely popular are the Eiffel Tower and Arc de Triomphe. Paris is famous for its beautifully maintained gardens and award-winning food.

Method — Look for descriptions of verbs or adjectives

1) Work through the passage <u>one sentence</u> at a time.
2) Look for places in a sentence where <u>verbs</u> or <u>adjectives</u> are <u>described</u>.

With millions of tourists each year, Paris is (easily) one of the most popular cities on Earth.

'easily' is an adverb — it changes the verb 'is'.

Two of the attractions that are (hugely) popular are the Eiffel Tower and Arc de Triomphe.

'hugely' is describing the adjective 'popular' — it's an adverb.

Paris is famous for its (beautifully) maintained gardens and award-winning food.

'beautifully' is describing how the gardens have been maintained. It's an adverb.

'award-winning' is not an adverb. It's describing 'food', which is a noun.

Practice Questions

1) Write down whether each option is a comparative, a superlative or just an adjective.

   a) funnier
   b) strangest
   c) most graceful
   d) bizarre
   e) joyful
   f) less fascinating

2) Underline the word in each sentence which matches the part of speech in brackets.

   a) Chris closed his eyes nervously as the shuttle started to move. (adverb)
   b) Joyce leant over to tell Aniela to try the crispy beef. (adjective)
   c) Molly looked around the building, but she couldn't find anything. (preposition)
   d) I was the only child waiting to be collected after school. (adjective)
   e) Carrie gladly accepted the offer of a place to stay. (adverb)
   f) When Mum shouted, Terry always crawled under the table and sulked. (preposition)

Remember, adverbs can describe verbs, adjectives or other adverbs...

If you're struggling to find the adverbs in a sentence, find the adjectives and verbs first. Then, have a look to see if their meaning is affected by any other words — these will be the adverbs.

Section One — Grammar

Determiners

There are lots of words which can be determiners, and they all have different jobs in a sentence.

Determiners tell you more about Nouns

1) Determiners are small words that go before nouns.
2) They can show whether a noun is specific or general.

This cardigan is too expensive. ⬅ This sentence is about a specific cardigan.

They didn't like those flowers. ⬅ This refers to several specific flowers.

I made some cookies for Gorka. ⬅ These could be any cookies.

Articles are a type of determiner

1) The words 'a', 'an' and 'the' are all articles.
2) Use 'a' and 'an' for general things and 'the' for specific things.

Use 'a' when the next word starts with a consonant sound, and 'an' when it starts with a vowel sound.

An old lady was shouting at her neighbour.

This could be any old lady.

I walked home after the party.

This is a specific party.

They show How Many things there are

Determiners can also tell you how many things there are.

Elijah has twelve pairs of shoes. ⬅ The word 'twelve' shows the number of pairs of shoes you're talking about.

The bus was several minutes late. ⬅ 'several' tells you how many minutes late the bus was.

Determiners also show who Owns something

1) Some determiners explain who something belongs to.
2) They're words like 'my', 'your' and 'our'.

Determiners are sometimes similar to possessive pronouns — try not to mix them up.

I let him borrow my notepad after he argued with your brother.

Our new dog ran off and lost its collar in the park. ⬅ The determiners tell you who owns the nouns in each sentence.

Their house is cold, so bring your woolly jumpers.

Section One — Grammar

Determiners

Practise spotting Determiners and identifying their Function

Circle all the determiners in each sentence below.

a) Larry brought two rulers and a pencil case from home.
b) My husband and I finished painting our house yesterday.
c) I was the youngest person on that train.
d) "These sandwiches are disgusting!" exclaimed one disgruntled customer.

Method — Start by finding all the nouns

1) Read each sentence carefully and look for all the nouns.
2) Then look for words that show whether a noun is specific or general, how many of the noun there is, or who the noun belongs to.

a) Larry brought (two) rulers and (a) pencil case from home.

The word 'two' tells you how many rulers Larry bought.
This could be any pencil case.

b) (My) husband and I finished painting (our) house yesterday.

'My' and 'our' tell you who the nouns ('husband' and 'house') belong to.

c) I was (the) youngest person on (that) train.

The words 'the' and 'that' refer to specific nouns ('person' and 'train').

d) "(These) sandwiches are disgusting!" exclaimed (one) disgruntled customer.

'These' refers to a specific group of sandwiches.
'one' tells you how many disgruntled customers were speaking.

Practice Questions

1) Circle the correct determiner to complete each sentence below.

a) *A / Several* goat stole my snowboard.
b) Ken put *one / our* muddy boots outside.
c) Have you locked *their / an* garage?
d) Liam ate *more / four* lollipops than you.

2) Underline all the determiners in this passage.

> Monty had been a farmer for twenty years. He'd spent his whole life in the small, remote village where he was born. This year, he was going to leave everything behind and move to the city.

Determiners show whether something is general or specific...

...and they can also show quantity and ownership. This makes it important to know how to recognise determiners correctly — they can affect the overall meaning of a sentence quite a bit.

Section One — Grammar

Sentences, Clauses and Phrases

Your sentences will be crystal clear if you revise how to use phrases and clauses properly.

Phrases and Clauses Add Information to a Sentence

Phrases and clauses are groups of words that are used to form sentences.

A Phrase Doesn't normally have a Verb...

A phrase doesn't usually contain a verb, and it doesn't make sense on its own.

> Jade wore her new purple dress. ← 'her new purple dress' is a phrase.

> Duncan put his hands in his pockets. ← 'in his pockets' is a phrase.

...But a Clause always Does

Unlike a phrase, a clause always contains a verb.

> Suzy listened to the radio while she brushed her teeth.

This is a clause. The verb is 'brushed'.

> Paul loves going to the beach when he visits the seaside.

This is also a clause. The verb is 'visits'.

Complex Sentences have Main and Subordinate Clauses

1) A complex sentence is made up of an important clause and one or more less important clauses.
2) The important clause is called the main clause. It makes sense on its own.
3) The other clauses are called subordinate clauses — they don't make sense without the main clause.

Subordinate clauses are also called dependent clauses.

> I cleaned the house while you were out.

This is the main clause — it makes sense on its own.

This is the subordinate clause — you need to read the main clause to understand what's happening.

> We're leaving early because we're tired.

4) The subordinate clause can be at the beginning, middle or end of the sentence.
5) Subordinate clauses often start with conjunctions. If the subordinate clause is at the beginning of the sentence, it is separated from the main clause with a comma.

Section One — Grammar

Sentences, Clauses and Phrases

Compound Sentences are made from Two Equal Clauses

1) A compound sentence is made of two main clauses joined by a conjunction like 'or' 'and' or 'but'.
2) Each clause would make sense as a sentence on its own.

Martin sat down on the beach.   He fell asleep on the sand.

Stick the two clauses together using a conjunction to make a compound sentence.

Martin sat down on the beach and he fell asleep on the sand.

A conjunction is a 'joining' word. There's more on p.18.

Relative Clauses give information about Nouns

1) A relative clause is a type of subordinate clause that gives extra information about a noun.
2) They usually start with a relative pronoun, such as 'that', 'which', 'who' or 'whose'.

The painting that she bought on holiday is beautiful.

This is a relative clause. It gives you some extra information about the noun — the painting.

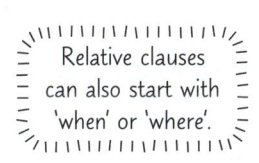

Relative clauses can also start with 'when' or 'where'.

Sometimes the Relative Pronoun is Left Out

1) Sometimes you can leave out the relative pronoun at the start of a relative clause.

Did you like the cake that I made you?

'that' is a relative pronoun.

Did you like the cake I made you?

This relative clause doesn't need a relative pronoun.

2) Sometimes you can't leave it out — the sentence won't make sense.

The tree which fell down was one hundred years old.

This sentence wouldn't make sense without the relative pronoun.

Adverbials act like Adverbs

1) An adverbial is any word or group of words that acts like an adverb.
2) They can describe why, when, where and how often something happens.

You should brush your teeth twice a day.

'twice a day' describes how often you should brush your teeth.

Yin played the violin in her bedroom.

'in her bedroom' describes where Yin played her violin.

3) Adverbials at the start of sentences are called fronted adverbials.

Before school, Rowan walked the dog.

Fronted adverbials usually have commas after them. There's more on p.33.

Section One — Grammar

Sentences, Clauses and Phrases

Preposition Phrases can tell you When or Where

1) A preposition phrase is a group of words which usually tell you when or where something or someone is.
2) Preposition phrases always start with a preposition.

> Some phrases are both a preposition phrase and an adverbial.

| Parents' Evening will take place next Thursday. | Phoebe left her wallet on the bedside table. |

'next' and 'on' are both prepositions.

Noun Phrases describe things

A noun phrase is a group of words which includes a noun and any words that describe it.

Noun phrases can include Adjectives

the sinister woman   the fat cat

Noun phrases can include Preposition Phrases

the cat on the rug   the vampire at the window

Noun phrases can include Other Nouns

the history teacher   a London bus   the Easter egg

Practise spotting Phrases, Main Clauses and Subordinate Clauses

EXAMPLE: Identify whether these are phrases, main clauses or subordinate clauses.
a) bright blue eyes   d) last Saturday night
b) Jane is late for work   e) after I finish my lunch
c) if you see a dolphin   f) let's go shopping

Method — Start by picking out the phrases

1) Start by finding the examples that don't have verbs. These are the phrases.

   a) bright blue eyes   d) last Saturday night   — a) and d) are both phrases — they add information to a sentence.

2) Then look for subordinate clauses — these won't make sense on their own.

   c) if you see a dolphin   e) after I finish my lunch   — c) and e) are subordinate clauses — they contain verbs but don't make sense on their own.

3) Finally look for main clauses — these can form sentences on their own.

   b) Jane is late for work   f) let's go shopping   — b) and f) are main clauses — they contain verbs and make sense on their own.

Section One — Grammar

Sentences, Clauses and Phrases

Make sure that you can **Recognise Sentence Types**

 Read this passage and then answer the questions that follow.

> Polar bears live in the Arctic. They are the largest land carnivores in the world and an adult male can weigh up to 700 kg. Polar bears typically hunt seals but they will also eat reindeer, walruses, birds, eggs and shellfish. The number of polar bears has declined in recent years due to hunting and loss of sea ice.

a) Write down a complex sentence from the passage.
b) Write down a compound sentence from the passage.
c) Write down a subordinate clause from the passage.

Method — Identify each sentence in the passage

Go through the passage and identify each sentence as you go along.

> Polar bears live in the Arctic. ← This sentence is a main clause. It isn't needed for the questions.

> They are the largest land carnivores in the world and an adult male can weigh up to 700 kg.

This is a compound sentence — it has two main clauses and a conjunction ('and'). This is one answer to b).

> Polar bears typically hunt for seals but they will also eat reindeer, walruses, birds, eggs and shellfish.

This is another compound sentence. It could also be the answer to part b).

> The number of polar bears has declined in recent years due to hunting and loss of sea ice.

This sentence is a complex sentence. The first part is a main clause and the second part is a subordinate clause. It's the answer to part a).   The second clause is the answer to part c).

Practice Questions

1) Underline the subordinate clause in each sentence below.
   a) Before I go to bed, I always brush my teeth.
   b) Although he loves his job, the gardener is retiring.
   c) Shakil can't go swimming because he's got an upset stomach.

2) Write down whether these sentences are compound sentences or complex sentences.
   a) After scoring a goal, the footballer ran away to celebrate.
   b) The weather was sunny and there were no clouds in the sky.
   c) We could play rounders or we could go swimming.

 **Practise spotting different sentence types...**
Find a book or newspaper and have a go at identifying the different types of phrases and clauses you've covered in this section — it will really help you get the hang of them.

Section One — Grammar

Conjunctions

Conjunctions are like glue — they join different parts of a text together.

Conjunctions Join Clauses and Sentences

1) Conjunctions join clauses together in a sentence.

> I haven't got my homework because my dog ate it.

> It was raining so Mohammed put up his umbrella.

2) Co-ordinating conjunctions are words like 'and', 'but' and 'or'.
   They join two main clauses together to make one sentence.

> You must arrive on time or the gates will be locked.

'or' links the two main clauses together.

3) Subordinating conjunctions are words like 'although', 'until' and 'because'.
   They join a main clause and a subordinate clause together.

> I won't set off until I'm ready.

> Although he'd reminded me, I still forgot his birthday.

Subordinating conjunctions can go at the start of sentences or between two clauses.

Since the subordinate clause in this sentence comes first, you need a comma here.

Conjunctions can be Words or Short Phrases

Conjunctions may be Single Words

These are words like 'so', 'if', 'and', 'but', 'while' and 'since'.

> Mum's going to do some baking and she would like you to help.

> Let's go for a walk today while the weather is nice.

Conjunctions may be Short Phrases

Some conjunctions are made up of more than one word.

> Wally wasn't sure where the exit was even though he had looked at the map.

> Nadine left her homework at school so that she wouldn't have to do it.

Some conjunctions Come in Pairs

Conjunctions like 'either' / 'or' and 'neither' / 'nor' are often used in pairs.

> He had to either stay with a friend or find a hotel.

> I tried neither the salmon nor the tuna.

Section One — Grammar

Conjunctions

You need to Know How to Use Conjunctions

 **Circle the most appropriate conjunction to complete each sentence.**

a) Olive's new puppy was a bundle of energy *because / but / whether / so* it certainly wasn't house-trained.

b) My bus was late again today *although / if / also / because* the driver had called in sick.

c) I'm really looking forward to the disco tonight *because / so / although / in case* I don't know what to wear.

Method — Look for the meaning of the sentence

1) Look for the <u>relationship</u> between the <u>two clauses</u> in each sentence. This gives the sentence its <u>meaning</u>.

2) Choose the best conjunction that fits the meaning of the sentence.

a) Olive's new puppy was a bundle of energy **but** it certainly wasn't house-trained.

The first clause gives a positive description of Olive's new puppy... ... whilst the second clause introduces a negative point. So 'but' is the most logical conjunction to use.

b) My bus was late again today **because** the driver had called in sick.

The first clause explains that the bus was late... ... and the second clause explains why. So use 'because' to introduce the explanation.

c) I'm really looking forward to the disco tonight **although** I don't know what to wear.

The first clause is a positive statement... ... but the second clause makes a negative point. 'although' is the most logical conjunction to use.

Practice Questions

1) Underline the conjunctions in the passage below.

> The Amazon Rainforest covers 40% of South America, although it has decreased in size. Humans have cut down the trees because they need wood for construction and space for farms and roads. Conservation efforts are under way to protect the rainforest and stop people from illegally cutting down the trees.

2) Circle the most appropriate conjunction to complete each sentence.

a) I often eat cereal for breakfast *as well as / as a result / either / but* I sometimes eat toast.

b) I'd like to go out to the Italian restaurant tonight, *although / therefore / because / so* Chinese is my favourite.

TEST TIP — **Try out different conjunctions to see which one fits best...**

If you're asked to choose the correct conjunction and aren't sure which one is correct, try putting each option in the sentence to see which one makes the most sense.

Section One — Grammar

Standard English and Formal Writing

Standard English is English that uses correct spelling, punctuation and grammar. You should always use it in your written work.

The Subject and the Verb must Agree

1) In Standard English, the verb has to agree with whoever's doing the action.

Miguel and Bushra was driving. should be ➡ Miguel and Bushra were driving.

If there's more than one person doing the action, the verb should be plural.

Avoid these Common Mistakes

1) Don't get confused by pronouns. 'Them' is a pronoun and 'those' is a determiner — it points something out.

Them children are very polite. should be ➡ Those children are very polite.

2) Be careful with 'that' and 'what' too. When you're talking about a noun that's already been mentioned, use 'that'.

The suit what she was wearing. should be ➡ The suit that she was wearing.

3) Dropping the 'ly' from the end of an adverb is usually non-Standard English.

He runs too slow. should be ➡ He runs too slowly.

Formal texts use Different language

1) Formal writing is used to write to someone you don't know or someone you show respect to.
2) Formal texts often use more complicated words and they don't use contracted forms.

informal writing ➡ The crook was never caught.   That isn't what I said.
formal writing ➡ The criminal was never caught.   That is not what I said.

The Subjunctive Form is used in formal texts

1) You might also see the subjunctive form in formal texts.

I insist that she stay in bed until she feels better. ⬅ In informal writing, you would say 'should stay' or 'stays'.

2) The subjunctive can be used in sentences about situations that aren't real.

If that was the case, I'd be able to go.   If that were the case, I would be able to go.

 informal sentence   subjunctive form

Section One — Grammar

Standard English and Formal Writing

Practise spotting the Features of Formal and Informal Writing

 Read the following sentences and write down whether they're examples of informal or formal writing.

a) He didn't want to admit that he was wrong.
b) They could've telephoned you first.
c) If I were in your position, I would try not to think about it.
d) The room was grotty — no one had cleaned it in months.

Method — Look closely at the choice of words and grammar

Read each sentence carefully, paying close attention to the words the writer has chosen.

a) He didn't want to admit that he was wrong.

'didn't' is the contracted form of 'did not'. Contracted forms aren't used in formal writing, so this sentence is informal.

b) They could've telephoned you first.

This is the contracted form of 'could have', so this sentence is also informal.

c) If I were in your position, I would try not to think about it.

'were' is the subjunctive form of the verb 'to be', so this sentence is an example of formal writing.

d) The room was grotty — no one had cleaned it in months.

The word 'grotty' isn't as formal as 'dirty' or 'unclean', so this sentence is informal.

Practice Questions

1) Read the sentences below. Underline the correct word to complete the sentence using Standard English.
   a) Kyra *were / was* angry because Leo had lied to her.
   b) My dad was singing *badly / bad* in the shower.
   c) "I think I *do / did* the right thing yesterday," said Marco.
   d) She doesn't like *them / those* sausage rolls.

2) Rewrite these sentences using more formal language.
   a) You've spoken to Esme about the car's engine?
   b) If I was stronger, I'd be able to lift the box.
   c) Berta thought it'd be exciting, but it wasn't.
   d) He demands that she apologises immediately.

Make sure you can recognise informal words...

Sometimes a sentence can use correct spelling, punctuation and grammar but still be informal because of the words it uses. It's important you can spot examples of informal language.

Section One — Grammar

Answering Grammar Questions

These pages cover the type of grammar questions that might crop up on the Multiple Choice paper.

Multiple Choice — finding the Best Word to Fit

1) Some grammar questions will ask you to choose a word or phrase to complete a sentence.
2) For each line, you'll be asked to choose the option that is correct and makes sense.
3) It might look like this:

In the test, the passages will be about 8-10 lines long.

In the passage below you need to choose the word, or group of words, which fits best and completes the sentence. The passage needs to make sense and be written in correct English. Mark the letter for the option you pick on your answer sheet.

1   There is   There are   They're   There's   Their   plans to build a new supermarket in
        A   B   C   D   E

2   Marchead town centre. The local shops don't do may have did suffer as more
                                              A   B   C   D   E

3   people use the supermarket. Moreover And However In other words Because,
                                    A   B   C   D   E

4   a final decision won't be made until a meeting with local residents on Monday.

Method — Read through the whole sentence carefully

Read each sentence to yourself, testing each option one at a time.

1) You need to select the correct introduction for the first sentence:

   > There are plans to build a new supermarket in Marchead town centre.

   'There are' is the correct option.
   'plans' is plural so you need to use
   'There are' instead of 'There is' or 'There's'.

   'There are' is option B, so you'd mark 'B' on your answer sheet.

   You'll need to look at the whole sentence to work out the answer.

2) The second sentence looks at a possible impact of the supermarket:

   > The local shops may suffer as more people use the supermarket.

   The shops have not already suffered and it is not certain that they will.
   The correct option to use is 'may' — option C.

3) You need to choose the correct word at the beginning of the third sentence:

   > However, a final decision won't be made until a meeting with local residents on Monday.

   There is a change in tone in this sentence.
   'However' is the correct option — option C.

   All of the other options would be used to expand on the point in the last sentence.

Section One — Grammar

Answering Grammar Questions

Multiple Choice — answering Grammar Questions

1) You may be asked grammar questions as part of your comprehension test. These questions will be about the way words or phrases are used in the passage.
2) You'll need to be able to identify specific parts of speech, but you'll be given options to choose from (see Section Five for more on comprehension questions).

EXAMPLE: Read the passage and then answer the following questions.

> 1 Before I was two years old, a circumstance happened which I have never forgotten. It was early in the spring; there had been a little frost in the night, and a light mist still hung over the plantations and meadows. I and the other colts were feeding at the lower part of the field when we heard, quite in the distance, what sounded like
> 5 the cry of dogs. The oldest of the colts raised his head, pricked his ears, and said, "There are the hounds!" and immediately cantered off followed by the rest of us to the upper part of the field, where we could look over the hedge and see several fields beyond. My mother and an old riding horse of our master's were also standing near, and seemed to know all about it.

From 'Black Beauty' by Anna Sewell

1) What type of word is 'colts' (lines 3 and 5)?

   A Adjective   **B** Preposition   **C** Noun   **D** Adverb   **E** Pronoun

2) What type of word is 'immediately' (line 6)?

   A Preposition   **B** Adverb   **C** Collective noun   **D** Adjective   **E** Verb

3) Which of these words is a preposition: 'It was early in the spring' (line 2)?

   A It   **B** was   **C** early   **D** in   **E** spring

Method — Look for evidence in the text

1) To answer question 1, read the surrounding text to see how the word 'colts' is used:

   > I and the other colts were feeding at the lower part of the field...
   >
   > The oldest of the colts raised his head, pricked his ears...

   These extracts help you to work out that the colts are animals. The word 'colts' must therefore be a noun — option C.

2) Do the same for question 2. Look at how the word 'immediately' is used:

   > ... and immediately cantered off...

   'cantered' is a verb, so 'immediately' is an adverb because it's describing how the action was done — option B.

3) Question 3 is a bit different — you only need to look at the words in the question.

   > It was early in the spring

   A preposition shows how things are related, usually in terms of time and place. In this case, the preposition is 'in' — option D.

Section One — Grammar

Answering Grammar Questions

These pages should help you to get your head around Standard Answer grammar questions.

Standard Answer — answering Grammar Questions

These questions are just like Multiple Choice comprehension questions, but there won't be any options to choose from — you'll have to pick out the correct parts of speech yourself.

EXAMPLE: Read the passage below and then answer the questions that follow.

> 1   The door led right into a large kitchen, which was full of smoke from one end to the other: the Duchess was sitting on a three-legged stool in the middle, nursing a baby; the cook was leaning over the fire, stirring a large cauldron which seemed to be full of soup.
>
> 5   "There's certainly too much pepper in that soup!" Alice said to herself, as well as she could for sneezing.
>
> There was certainly too much of it in the air. Even the Duchess sneezed occasionally; and as for the baby, it was sneezing and howling alternately without a moment's pause. The only two creatures in the kitchen that did not sneeze,
>
> 10   were the cook, and a large cat, which was lying on the hearth and grinning from ear to ear.
>
> "Please would you tell me," said Alice, a little timidly, for she was not quite sure whether it was good manners for her to speak first, "why your cat grins like that?"
>
> 15   "It's a Cheshire-Cat," said the Duchess, "and that's why. Pig!"
>
> She said the last word with such sudden violence that Alice quite jumped; but she saw in another moment that it was addressed to the baby, and not to her, so she took courage, and went on again: —
>
> "I didn't know that Cheshire-Cats always grinned; in fact, I didn't know
>
> 20   that cats could grin."
>
> "They all can," said the Duchess; "and most of 'em do."

From 'Alice's Adventures in Wonderland' by Lewis Carroll

1) Give one example of each of the following parts of speech in this sentence taken from the passage.

   "Please would you tell me," said Alice, a little timidly, for she was not quite sure whether it was good manners for her to speak first, "why your cat grins like that?"

   a) a proper noun   **c)** a common noun
   b) a conjunction   **d)** an adverb

2) Who is the pronoun 'she' referring to in line 16?

3) Is the verb in 'it was addressed to the baby' (line 17) active or passive? Explain your answer.

Section One — Grammar

Answering Grammar Questions

Method — Read the text very carefully

1) To answer question 1, look carefully for each <u>part of speech</u>:

'Alice' is the only proper noun in the sentence. So 'Alice' is the answer to part a).

'for' is a conjunction in this sentence — it continues the sentence and explains why Alice spoke timidly. It could be the answer to part b).

> "Please would you tell me," said Alice, a little timidly, for she was not quite sure whether it was good manners for her to speak first, "why your cat grins like that?"

'whether' is a conjunction — it could answer part b).

'manners' and 'cat' are the only two common nouns in this sentence. Either could be the answer to part c).

'timidly', 'not', 'quite' and 'first' are adverbs because they describe verbs, adjectives or other adverbs.

2) For question 2, look at the <u>line before</u> line 16 to work out <u>who</u> is speaking.

> "It's a Cheshire-Cat," said the Duchess, "and that's why. Pig!"
> She said the last word with such sudden violence that Alice quite jumped;

The Duchess is speaking here, so it is the Duchess being referred to as 'she' in line 14.

Be careful — Alice is the only character named in the line, so you could be tricked into thinking that 'she' refers to her.

3) To work out whether 'it was addressed' is <u>active</u> or <u>passive</u>, read the text around it.

> she saw in another moment that it was addressed to the baby

The verb is focusing on the action, rather than the person doing it, so the sentence is passive.

Practice Questions

1) Read the passage below and then answer the questions that follow.

> 1 Harriet was desperate not to be distracted again. She'd already been trying to do her Maths homework for two hours and she had to get it finished before she could go out and play. Unfortunately, she could hear an incessant buzzing noise, and it was really putting her off. Angrily, she hauled herself to her feet and started to search
> 5 her bedroom for the culprit. The noise was coming from near the window...

   a) Find a conjunction used in line 3 of the passage.

   b) What part of speech is 'desperate' (line 1)?

   c) What part of speech is 'angrily' (line 4)?

You might need to look around for clues...

It's tempting to only focus on the line or part of the passage that you're being asked about in the question, but you might need to search elsewhere in the passage to find the correct answer.

Section One — Grammar

Practice Questions

Well done — you've reached the end of the grammar section. Before you move on to the next section, check how well you remember this one by having a go at these practice questions.

> Underline the correct pronoun to complete each sentence. Look at this example:
>
> **Example:** Max asked Jane how he could help (she I <u>her</u>).

1. I lost my purse, but luckily Zac found (**them   it   him**).

2. She had an argument with her parents and is refusing to speak to (**they   it   them**).

3. We both made a salad — they loved his but they didn't like (**ours   his   mine**).

4. Charlie wanted to stroke the cat, but it hissed at (**him   he   his**).

5. Ahil and I are going to the funfair — (**we   she   I**) are very excited.

> The underlined verb in each sentence has been used incorrectly. Write the correct form of the verb on the line. Look at this example:
>
> **Example:** We are <u>gone</u> to the beach now.   *going*

6. Mei suggested that we <u>went</u> to the cinema to watch that film. _____

7. They will be <u>travelled</u> around the world to mark their retirement. _____

8. Who <u>are</u> you talking to on the telephone earlier? _____

9. I don't <u>remembered</u> which school you went to. _____

10. We haven't <u>spot</u> anything unusual in his behaviour so far. _____

Section One — Grammar

Practice Questions

> Underline the word in each sentence that matches the part of speech in brackets. Look at this example:
>
> **Example:** They saw a large toad <u>in</u> the pond. **(preposition)**

11. It was an extremely hot day, so we stayed at home. **(adverb)**

12. Sally was overjoyed at the news that she had won the competition. **(adjective)**

13. I looked through the window and saw them playing volleyball. **(preposition)**

14. Adam hopped over the gate and landed in a deep puddle. **(adjective)**

15. The poorly calf was feeding well after being reunited with its mother. **(adverb)**

16. Annoyingly, my train was delayed by a signal failure. **(preposition)**

> Underline the correct determiner in the brackets to complete each sentence. Look at this example:
>
> **Example:** There was (**<u>one</u>**   five   those) child at the bus stop.

17. (**Wild   This   Those**) horses can gallop faster than the others.

18. I would rather have an ice cream than (**some   drink   these**) bitter lemonade.

19. Alisha couldn't believe (**her   the   my**) eyes when she saw a lion in the garden.

20. After the hike, (**our   every   that**) legs were aching a lot.

21. They had read (**their   those   all**) of the books in the small library.

Section One — Grammar

Practice Questions

> Write down whether the part of each sentence that is underlined is an adverbial or a noun phrase. Look at this example:
>
> **Example:** The ecstatic toddler jumped up and down. _adverbial_

22. The people who live next door play loud music all day. _____

23. Claudia is bored, so she wants to leave tomorrow morning. _____

24. The intrepid explorer trekked deeper into the jungle. _____

25. She goes to the dentist every six months. _____

26. As quietly as possible, I crept out from my hiding place. _____

27. A village close to Gloucester has been without power for days. _____

> Underline the most appropriate conjunction to complete each sentence. Look at this example:
>
> **Example:** I'll go shopping, (since because <u>although</u>) I don't want to.

28. Hasan made dinner (**and neither but**) did the washing-up.

29. She kept thinking about (**but because whether**) he had lost his way.

30. Dylan was greeted warmly (**as although until**) he arrived very late.

31. It's a poor result (**however either so**) you look at it.

32. I discovered a pleasant path (**although since while**) I was out jogging.

Section One — Grammar

Practice Questions

> Underline the correct word from the brackets to complete each sentence below using Standard English. Look at this example:
>
> **Example:** You (talks <u>talk</u> talking talker) a lot.

33. He laughed really (**noisy** **noisily** **noise** **noisiest**) in the playground.

34. They (**is** **be** **was** **were**) thrilled about the result of the match.

35. (**Them** **Those** **Theirs** **That**) cats are noisy, especially at night.

36. The apple (**what** **that** **when** **how**) he ate was rotten.

37. She held the bird very (**careful** **gently** **good** **proper**).

> Underline the most appropriate word from the brackets to complete the sentence. Look at this example:
>
> **Example:** Naomi (delivers <u>delivered</u> delivering) the wrong parcel yesterday.

38. There were (**several** **more** **many**) unread books on his shelf than mine.

39. Naira was told off (**although** **whenever** **unless**) she argued with her brother.

40. The fruit bowl was placed (**through** **over** **on**) the coffee table.

41. He asked me how I was but I did not know what to tell (**him** **he** **his**).

42. I had (**sleep** **sleeping** **slept**) for seven hours when I suddenly woke up.

43. I ate my dinner very (**quick** **quickly** **quicker**).

Section One — Grammar

Section Two — Punctuation

Starting and Ending Sentences

Sentences can be tricky to understand when punctuation marks are missing.

Start each sentence with a Capital Letter...

For the start of a sentence, there's just one very simple rule.
Whatever you ended the last sentence with, always *start* the next with a *capital letter*.

My friend Holly loves the summer. **S**he always eats ice cream.

↙ capital letter at the start   ↙ another capital letter for a new sentence

The skyscraper has forty-six floors. **I**t is a very tall building.

...End with a Full Stop, Exclamation Mark, Question Mark or Ellipsis

You've got *four options* at the *end* of a sentence. You usually need a *full stop*, but you might use a *question mark*, *exclamation mark* or *ellipsis* instead.
Make sure you know when and how to use each one...

A Full Stop goes at the end of a Sentence

If you're just writing an *ordinary sentence*, use a full stop.

Filip put the parcel up to his ear and shook it gently**.** It rattled**.** ⇐ another full stop

↑ a full stop

An Exclamation Mark shows Strong Feelings

1) Use an exclamation mark to show strong feelings like *fear*, *anger* or *surprise*.

   Ouch, that was my foot**!** ⇐ This exclamation mark shows shock and pain.

   That's a scary spider**!** ⇐ This exclamation mark shows fear.

   I am furious**!** ⇐ This exclamation mark shows anger.

2) Exclamation marks can also show someone *shouting* or giving a *command*.

   Don't run**!** ⇐ This exclamation mark shows a command.

   Hello there**!** ⇐ This exclamation mark shows that someone is shouting.

   Try not to use too many exclamation marks in your writing. It makes you sound over the top.

Section Two — Punctuation

Starting and Ending Sentences

A **Question Mark** goes at the end of a **Question**

1) Question marks are only for sentences that actually ask a question.

> What time is it**?** ← You need a question mark here.

2) Don't put them at the end of sentences that just tell you about a question.

> She asked what time it was**.** ← **no** question mark here

An **Ellipsis** leaves a sentence **Hanging**

1) If you want to deliberately leave a sentence unfinished, you can use an ellipsis (three dots). This can be good for adding suspense to a story.

> It had seemed like such a good idea, but**...** ← This ellipsis could be used at the end of a chapter to add suspense.

2) They're also a good way to show interrupted speech.

> "Valeska! Er, I was just**...**"

You might be asked to **Split Up** a passage into **Sentences**

 This paragraph is missing full stops and capital letters. Rewrite the passage so that it is correctly split into sentences.

> tigers, lions and cheetahs are all part of the big cat family tigers live in Asia, and are jungle animals lions and cheetahs both live on the plains of Africa

Method — Where you take a big breath, put a full stop

1) You know that the first word is the start of a sentence, so it needs a capital T.
2) Now read the passage through (aloud if that helps) and put in a full stop and capital letter each time you take a big breath. This is where you start a new point.

capital letter at the start →   big breath →

> **T**igers, lions and cheetahs are all part of the big cat family**. T**igers live in Asia, and are jungle animals**. L**ions and cheetahs both live on the plains of Africa**.**

↑ big breath   ↑ Don't forget the full stop at the end.

Section Two — Punctuation

Starting and Ending Sentences

You should also be able to **Spot Mistakes** in a passage

 In this passage there are some mistakes in the use of capital letters and punctuation. On each numbered line there is either one mistake or no mistake. Draw a circle around each mistake.

1	"Let's go to Millom" cried Sammy excitedly.
2	Harry sighed because they always went to Millom on Sammy's birthday.
3	"Are you sure?" asked Harry. "wouldn't you rather go to Windermere?"

Method — Check the passage line by line

1) Line 1 has speech showing strong emotion, so it should have an exclamation mark.

See p.38 for rules on writing speech.

2) There are no mistakes in Line 2. It starts with a capital letter and ends with a full stop. And it doesn't have anything fancy, like speech, to catch you out.

3) Line 3 has two sentences in it, so check each sentence separately:

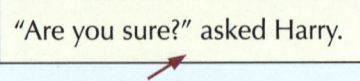   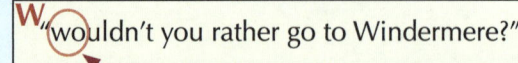

This bit's fine...   ...but this is a new sentence, so it needs a capital letter.

Practice Questions

1) Rewrite these sentences, adding the correct punctuation to start and end each one.
   a) look out — it's the mutant cheesecake   b) does this hat make my ears look funny

2) Write a sentence to show the correct use of:
   a) an ellipsis.   b) a question mark.   c) an exclamation mark.   d) a full stop.

3) In this passage there are some mistakes in the use of capital letters and punctuation. Each line has one mistake or no mistakes. Rewrite the passage with no mistakes.

1	Peter Handy was a fisherman. Every day he went out on his boat in the bay to
2	catch fish. One day he went down to the dock as usual to find his boat missing?
3	"Oh dear!" cried Peter. "What am I going to do now"
4	He sat down on the dock and put his head in his hands. But just then?

Use ellipses to build tension...

Remember that ellipses can be used to show interrupted speech as well as to add suspense to a text. You can normally tell which way they're being used from the context of the sentence.

Section Two — Punctuation

Commas, Dashes and Brackets

Some sentences, like this one, sound a lot better if commas are used correctly.

Commas Separate parts of a Sentence

Here are some examples of when you should use a comma in a sentence:

A comma Separates Items in a List

1) A list that doesn't contain any commas is really hard to understand.

   I love ice cream cake sandwiches and chips.

2) Put a comma after each item in the list to break up the sentence:

   I love ice cream, cake, sandwiches and chips.

   Add commas here.

   Put 'and' or 'or' between the last two items in a list. Remember, you don't need to use a comma before 'and' or 'or'.

A comma helps to Avoid Ambiguity

1) Some sentences can be ambiguous — this means that it's not clear exactly what the sentence is trying to say.

2) You can use commas to avoid ambiguity or change the meaning of a sentence.

   Alpacas which have fluffy coats are very friendly.

   This suggests that only alpacas with fluffy coats are very friendly.

   Alpacas, which have fluffy coats, are very friendly.

   This tells you that all alpacas are very friendly and have fluffy coats.

A comma comes after Fronted Adverbials and Subordinate Clauses

When a fronted adverbial or a subordinate clause comes at the beginning of a sentence, you need to separate it from the rest of the sentence using a comma.

   With a scream, Ilana turned on the light.

   This is an adverbial phrase, so it needs a comma.

   Before she turned on the light, Ilana screamed.

   This is a subordinate clause.

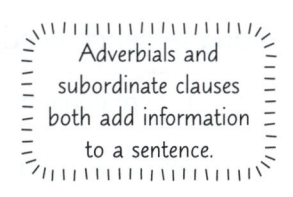

Adverbials and subordinate clauses both add information to a sentence.

Section Two — Punctuation

Commas, Dashes and Brackets

Commas, Brackets and Dashes also Separate Extra Information

Brackets bring Extra Information into a sentence

Add brackets around extra information to keep it separate:

My friend Zara is really good at football (unlike me). *You don't need to know this to understand the sentence.*

Carly and Adam (who are both 14) are going shopping.

Brackets should always be used in pairs.

Commas and Dashes can be used Instead of Brackets

1) You can add a pair of dashes or commas around extra information to keep it separate.

   The best thing my mum can cook — if she can cook anything — is beans on toast.

   These carrots, freshly picked this morning, are going to make a delicious soup.

2) A single dash can also join together two related main clauses.

   I peered into the shed — Mary's old violin was on a shelf on the back wall.

You might be asked to Add Punctuation to a Passage

EXAMPLE: This extract is missing some punctuation. Rewrite the extract, adding commas, dashes and brackets where they are needed.

> Romy Julie and the twins who had just turned 5 were going to the airport. The children were contemplating their first flight they had terrified looks on their faces. With a kind smile Julie told them not to worry.

Method — Check for lists and extra information

1) The first sentence has a list and extra information which needs to be separated:

   Romy, Julie and the twins (who had just turned 5) were going to the airport.

   Comma needed here to break up the list.   *A pair of brackets, commas or dashes is needed here.*

2) The second sentence needs a single dash to separate the two clauses:

   The children were contemplating their first flight — they had terrified looks on their faces.

   You could also have put brackets around the second part of the sentence.

3) In the third sentence, 'With a kind smile' is a fronted adverbial — it needs a comma:

   With a kind smile, Julie told them not to worry.

Commas, Dashes and Brackets

Some questions may ask you to **Spot Punctuation Errors**

EXAMPLE: Circle the errors in the use of commas and brackets in the passage below.

> 1 Max (my cousin) was desperate, to visit the zoo at half-term.
> 2 He really wanted to see the lions, giraffes, tigers, and monkeys.
> 3 When he arrived at 4pm it was a long drive Max heard that the tiger was ill.

Method — Read each sentence out to yourself

1) Start by reading Line 1 aloud. There is extra punctuation that shouldn't be there.

   Max (my cousin) was desperate, to visit the zoo at half-term.

   The brackets are right — they separate the information.
   This comma is wrong — it's in the middle of a clause.

2) Then move on to Line 2. Not every item in the list needs a comma after it:

   He really wanted to see the lions, giraffes, tigers, and monkeys.

   These two commas are right — they split up the list.
   This comma is not needed.

3) Then read out Line 3. This one is different — it needs punctuation adding to it:

   When he arrived at 4pm (it was a long drive), Max heard that the tiger was ill.

   Brackets separate the extra information.
   A comma is needed after the bracket to separate the subordinate clause.

Practice Questions

1) Rewrite each sentence, adding commas to make each one correct.
   a) Eddie the newest addition to the family was just three days old.
   b) Ravens pigeons and seagulls were Nicci's least favourite types of bird.
   c) Although they couldn't hear George shouted angrily at the boys as they ran away.

2) There are ten errors in the use of commas and brackets in the passage below. Rewrite the paragraph using the correct punctuation.

   Each bracket in the pair counts as one error.

   > Ram, and Lucy were sick of their P.E. teacher Mr Oden. Every day he made them do high jump, shot-put, rugby (and football). One day they came up with a cunning plan along with the other children to get revenge on Mr Oden. They took all of the studs out, of his football boots they stole them from under his desk so that when he put them on and started running he fell head first into the mud.

There are three types of punctuation for adding more information...

Brackets or dashes can often be used instead of commas to add extra information to a sentence, but sometimes you have to use a comma — e.g. after a fronted adverbial or subordinate clause.

Section Two — Punctuation

Apostrophes and Hyphens

It's easy to get muddled with apostrophes — luckily these pages explain what you need to know.

Apostrophes show Possession...

1) When you're writing about who owns what, add an apostrophe to the noun:

My dog's dinner

My dogs' dinner

The children's dinner

The noun is singular (there's one dog). Add an apostrophe + 's'.

The noun is plural and ends in 's' (there's more than one dog). Add an apostrophe after the 's'.

The noun is plural but doesn't end in 's'. Add an apostrophe + 's'.

...and where a Contracted Form has been made

1) Apostrophes are used to make contracted forms of words.
2) You add an apostrophe where letters have been removed.

We're all off on holiday. When you write 'we're' instead of 'we are', the apostrophe shows where 'a' has been left out.

Contracted forms are sometimes called 'contractions.'

3) Here are some common contracted forms:

| I am → I'm | I would → I'd | they are → they're | does not → doesn't |
| I will not → I won't | I had → I'd | who is → who's | can not → can't |

It's is the Contracted Form of It Is or It Has

1) 'It's' with an apostrophe is always short for 'it is' or 'it has'.

It's raining outside. It is raining outside.   It's been raining for days. It has been raining for days.

If you're not sure whether to use 'its' or 'it's', see whether the sentence would make sense with 'it is' or 'it has' instead.

2) 'Its' means something belongs to it. It never has an apostrophe.

Have you fed the dog its dinner?   The team has won its match.

Use Hyphens to Avoid Confusion

1) Hyphens can be used in phrases to show which word is being described.

Fakhir has just seen a man-eating shark. With the hyphen, this means a shark that eats people. Without the hyphen, it means a man who was eating a shark.

2) Some prefixes also use hyphens.

co-owner   ex-partner   self-confidence

Section Two — Punctuation

Apostrophes and Hyphens

Make sure that you can Add Apostrophes to Text

EXAMPLE: This extract is missing some apostrophes. Rewrite the extract, adding the apostrophes where they are needed.

> Michelles horse is called Pansy and its amazing how lazy she is.
> Shes always looking for food and she wont move a muscle if its been raining.
> Pansys vet is going to do some tests to make sure that she isnt ill.

Method — Look for possession and short forms of words

Read through <u>each line</u>. Look closely for places where apostrophes <u>may be needed</u>.

Michelle's horse is called Pansy and it's amazing how lazy she is.

- An apostrophe is needed here — the horse belongs to Michelle.
- This is the short form of 'it is', so add an apostrophe here.

She's always looking for food and she won't move a muscle if it's been raining.

- This is short for 'she is'. Add an apostrophe here.
- This is the short form of 'will not'.
- Add an apostrophe here — this means 'it has'.

Pansy's vet is going to do some tests to make sure that she isn't ill.

- Add an apostrophe here. The vet belongs to Pansy.
- 'tests' is a plural noun so you don't need an apostrophe here.
- This is the short form of 'is not', so add an apostrophe here.

Practice Questions

1) These sentences are each missing an apostrophe.
   Rewrite the sentences, adding the apostrophes where they are needed.
   a) Megan's goalkeeper jersey wasnt going to dry in time for her match.
   b) "There's no way that you're going out when its this cold," shouted Zac's mum.
   c) Beatrice suddenly realised that she'd left her homework at her dads house.
   d) The mens boots were covered in mud from the garden.

2) Some of the sentences below need one or more hyphens to avoid confusion.
   Using the information in brackets, decide whether each sentence needs any hyphens.
   a) Claudia bought an orange striped teapot.   (a teapot with orange stripes)
   b) The four year old children were playing in the sand.   (children aged four)
   c) The pile of well folded clothes fell onto the floor.   (clothes folded well)
   d) My cousin collects little polished ornaments.   (small ornaments that are polished)

Apostrophes and hyphens are used to make things clearer...

Make sure you understand what they show, and when you should use them in your writing.

Section Two — Punctuation

Speech

There's nothing scary about inverted commas — you just have to use them in the right places.

Inverted Commas show when someone is Speaking

1) You need to use inverted commas when you quote direct speech — the actual words someone speaks. The inverted commas go before and after the spoken words.

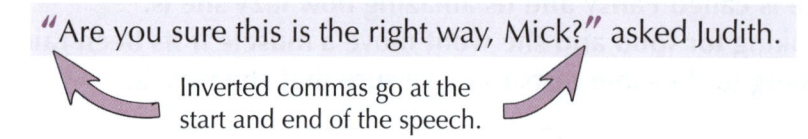

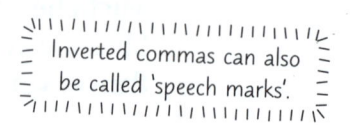

"Are you sure this is the right way, Mick?" asked Judith.

Inverted commas go at the start and end of the speech.

Inverted commas can also be called 'speech marks'.

2) You should only use inverted commas if you quote exactly what someone has said.

Judith asked Mick if he was sure that it was the right way.

There's no actual speech in this sentence, so you don't need inverted commas.

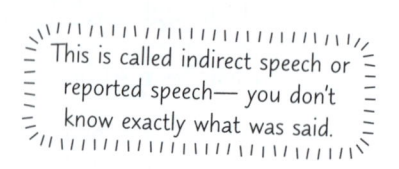

This is called indirect speech or reported speech— you don't know exactly what was said.

Speech always ends with a Punctuation Mark

There are four rules that you need to know:

1) Use a Comma if the Sentence Continues after the speech ends

"Let's go on the roller coaster," suggested Dwayne.

The sentence continues after the speech, so add a comma.

2) Use a Full Stop if the Sentence Ends when the speech ends

Soheila said, "I'd love to go hiking."

The sentence ends here, so you need a full stop.

This comma introduces the speech.

3) Use an Exclamation Mark if the speech shows Strong Feelings

"Tidy your room!" yelled Sam.

Sam is shouting, so it needs an exclamation mark.

4) Use a Question Mark if the speech is a Question

"Where are you going?" asked Alia.

This is a question, so it needs a question mark.

Section Two — Punctuation

Speech

You may have to Add Inverted Commas to Text

EXAMPLE: Rewrite this passage, adding inverted commas where they are needed.

> Mum, can we get a puppy? asked Laura, for the sixth time that week.
> Laura's mum sighed, Who would take it for a walk?
> Laura spent the next five minutes telling her mum how she'd have time to do it.

Method — Look for quoted speech in the passage

1) Work through the passage <u>one sentence</u> at a time.
2) Make sure that you only add inverted commas to words that <u>someone has said</u>.

"Mum, can we get a puppy?" asked Laura, for the sixth time that week.

These are the actual words Laura says to her mum, so they need inverted commas.

Laura's mum sighed, "Who would take it for a walk?"

Laura's mum is asking a question here, so this needs inverted commas.

3) Remember that you <u>don't</u> need inverted commas for <u>reported speech</u>.

Laura spent the next five minutes telling her mum how she'd have time to do it.

This isn't Laura's actual speech, so it doesn't need inverted commas.

Practice Questions

1) Write down the sentence in each pair that has been punctuated correctly.
   a) "Listen carefully," said Matt, as he told them about the "wizard's warning". OR
      "Listen carefully," said Matt, as he told them about the wizard's warning.
   b) Alex screamed into the night air, "Why can't I find the way"? OR
      Alex screamed into the night air, "Why can't I find the way?"
   c) I need "three starters, two desserts and one drink," shouted the waiter. OR
      "I need three starters, two desserts and one drink," shouted the waiter.

2) The sentences below are missing inverted commas.
   Rewrite the sentences, adding inverted commas where they are needed.

   a) How many people are coming? asked Giles.
   b) Helen asked, Will you have time to visit Maggie, Jurgen? I'm too busy.
   c) Take some sun cream! shouted Heidi. It's sweltering out there.

Remember to put punctuation inside speech marks...

It's important that you correctly punctuate any bits of speech — if the speech needs a question mark or an exclamation mark, put that punctuation inside the inverted commas (not outside).

Colons and Semicolons

You're nearly there for punctuation — just colons and semicolons left to revise.

Colons and Semicolons Add Information to Sentences

Colons Introduce Lists and Explanations

1) You can use a colon to show that a list is about to begin:

This bit before the colon should make sense on its own. → You will need several items: a tennis racket, tennis balls, a T-shirt, shorts, socks and trainers. ← The colon goes here, just before the list begins.

2) Colons can also show that you're about to explain a point you've just made. They normally separate two main clauses:

The office was empty: everyone had finished work and gone home. ← This is the explanation — it's explaining why the office was empty.

Add a colon here, before the explanation.

Semicolons Join Clauses and Break Up Lists

1) Semicolons are used to join two sentences into one. The sentences must be about the same thing and equally important.

There's more about clauses on page 14.

You're going to see him tomorrow; you'll know more then.

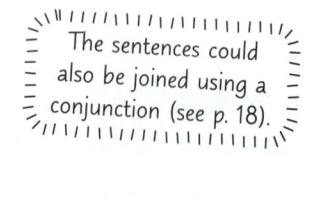

The sentences could also be joined using a conjunction (see p. 18).

The semicolon joins the two sentences together.

2) Semicolons are also used to break up lists of long phrases or clauses.

In 2008, the fête had stalls selling cakes; in 2009, there was a 'guess the number of sweets in the jar' competition; and in 2010, the local children danced round a maypole.

You need a semicolon before the 'and'.

Colons and Semicolons are used Differently

Remember that a colon offers an explanation of what comes before it, but a semicolon doesn't.

Liam is happy; Esau has baked a cake.

The semicolon implies that the two clauses are related — it suggests that Liam's happiness and Esau's baking might have the same cause or that the two things happened at the same time.

Liam is happy: Esau has baked a cake.

The colon shows that Liam is happy because Esau has baked a cake.

Section Two — Punctuation

Colons and Semicolons

Practise **Adding Colons** and **Semicolons** to **Sentences**

EXAMPLE: Add one colon or semicolon to each line so that the punctuation is correct.
- a) You need to buy several items 4 eggs, 300 g of flour and 200 g of sugar.
- b) Kyle is on holiday this week German class will go ahead as usual.
- c) Mr Smith was furious I'd forgotten my homework again.

Method — Find lists, clauses and explanations

1) Find the place in each sentence where a colon or semicolon could be added.
2) Don't confuse colons and semicolons — look back at the last page if you're not sure.

a) You need to buy several items: 4 eggs, 300 g of flour and 200 g of sugar.

A colon goes here, before the start of the list of ingredients.

The items in this list are short phrases, so you use a colon but no semicolons.

b) Kyle is on holiday this week; German class will go ahead as usual.

The two clauses are related, but the second clause isn't an explanation or a definition. So you need to use a semicolon.

c) Mr Smith was furious: I'd forgotten my homework again.

Add a colon here. This part of the sentence explains why Mr Smith was furious.

Practice Questions

1) There are three errors in the use of colons and semicolons in this passage. Find the errors and write the passage out again.

> Pierre was very excited: it was the end of term. He was going to Greece on holiday the very next day. Pierre was looking forward to swimming in the bright blue sea: browsing the local Greek markets, looking for souvenirs; playing tennis at the hotel and paying a visit to Athens. He didn't want to go to any museums: his mum would probably make him go anyway.

2) Each of these sentences is missing at least one semicolon. Rewrite each sentence and add the missing semicolons.

You may need to add more than one semicolon to the sentences.

- a) I've worked really hard I expect to pass my exams.
- b) I never miss a football match I'm the top scorer in the team.
- c) I went to the market for a new hat, but they didn't have any I'll be back on Monday.
- d) I would like to thank my mum, who inspired me to sing my teacher, who taught me how to hit the high notes and my partner, who wrote me some great songs.

TEST TIP — Write punctuation marks carefully...

Colons and semicolons look similar — make sure it's clear which one you use in the test.

Section Two — Punctuation

Answering Punctuation Questions

Questions in the real test can be a punctuation minefield — these pages will help you answer them.

Multiple Choice — finding punctuation mistakes

1) If you're taking a Multiple Choice paper, you might get a question asking you to find the punctuation mistakes in a short passage.
2) For each line, you'll be asked to identify if there's a mistake; and if there is, you'll need to say where in the line the mistake is.
3) It might look a bit like this:

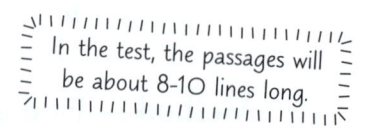

In the test, the passages will be about 8-10 lines long.

EXAMPLE: There are some punctuation errors in this passage. In each line there is either one mistake or no mistake. Find the group of words with the mistake in it and mark its letter on your answer sheet. If there is no mistake, mark N.

1 Will you do something amazing today? Read on to learn more. Drought
   A   B   C   D   N

2 victims are in desperate need of food; water and other essential items.
   A   B   C   D   N

3 Any money (no matter how little) can make a difference? Please help us.
   A   B   C   D   N

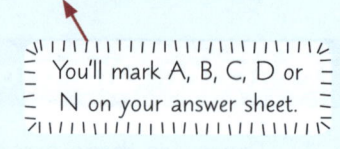

You'll mark A, B, C, D or N on your answer sheet.

Method — Check the passage line by line

Read the passage through once before you write anything, then read it line by line. Check that the punctuation in the line is correct, then check if any punctuation is missing.

1) Line 1 has no mistakes in it, so the answer is N.
2) Line 2 looks fairly simple until you get to the middle where there's a semicolon.

> victims are in desperate need of food**;** water and other essential items.

The mistake is in part C — the list contains short items, so they don't need to be separated by a semicolon. Use a comma instead.

3) Line 3 has two sentences that you need to check.

> Any money (no matter how little) can make a difference**?** Please help us.

This isn't a question, so it's wrong to use a question mark here — the answer is C.

This sentence is fine.

Section Two — Punctuation

Answering Punctuation Questions

Standard Answer — adding the Correct Punctuation

1) If you're taking a Standard Answer paper, your question will be slightly different.
2) You'll be given a passage with mistakes in (or no punctuation at all) which you'll need to rewrite with the correct punctuation. It might look a bit like this:

EXAMPLE: Add the missing punctuation to the passage below.

> **Nishi was furious with Ronald her next-door neighbour he kept shouting at the top of his voice playing loud music and kicking footballs against her bedroom window she opened her window one day caught the football and refused to give it back you can have it back when you learn to grow up she shouted.**
>
> *(10 marks)*

Use the number of marks as a guide, but remember that there's usually more than one mistake per mark.

Method — Think about how you would say it

Read the passage through once before you start correcting the mistakes.
Then read it again really slowly, thinking about where you'd need natural pauses if you were saying the passage out loud (try to get used to doing this in your head).

1) Write down the first sentence — you need to work out where it ends.

   | Nishi was furious with Ronald her next door neighbour. He kept |

   This needs a full stop in order for the passage to make sense.

   You could add a colon instead of a full stop, because the next bit explains why Nishi was furious.

2) Now you've created a sentence, think about whether it needs anything else.

   These sound like two separate bits, so you need to split them up.

   | Nishi was furious with Ronald | (her next-door neighbour). |

   Brackets split up the sentence nicely, but you could also use a comma.

   There might be more than one way to add punctuation to a sentence.

   | Nishi was furious with Ronald, her next-door neighbour. |

   For more on when to use brackets, see p.34.

Practise until you can punctuate perfectly...

REVISION TIP: Revising punctuation can seem a bit dull, but it's worth doing. You'd kick yourself if you lost marks on a question because you forgot to punctuate a couple of sentences correctly.

Section Two — Punctuation

Practice Questions

You've made it to the end of the punctuation section, so it's time to put the skills you've been revising to the test. If you're struggling with a particular question, look back at the relevant page.

> Complete each sentence by writing the most suitable of a full stop, an exclamation mark, a question mark or an ellipsis on the line. Look at this example:
>
> **Example:** What are you going to do this weekend __?__

1. We are so excited to see you _____

2. Giraffes have long necks to reach the highest leaves _____

3. She was creeping past the entrance to the lair, when suddenly _____

4. Where can we find a baker to make such a large pie _____

5. Don't eat that — it's poisonous _____

> Write down whether each sentence uses commas correctly or incorrectly. Look at this example:
>
> **Example:** When we phoned, there was no answer. __correct__

6. Lobsters which have big claws, live on the ocean floor. _____

7. I went to the supermarket to buy apples, bananas and pears. _____

8. She relaxed into the comfortable armchair, with a sigh. _____

9. Kemal, who is seven years old, loves playing football. _____

10. We bought a set of pencils pens, a sharpener and a glue stick. _____

Section Two — Punctuation

Practice Questions

> Add a pair of brackets to complete each sentence. Look at this example:
>
> **Example:** The shop **(** open between 9am and 6pm **)** sells shoes .

11. Lancaster a city in the north of England has a medieval castle .

12. Ron who speaks Italian arranged the trip to Venice in the summer .

13. When they arrive assuming they do we'll ask why they're late .

14. Oliver and Laurissa both sales assistants took ballet classes .

15. The stories he told there were many fascinated the children .

> Each of these sentences is missing an apostrophe. Rewrite the incorrect word in each sentence with the apostrophe in the correct place. Look at this example:
>
> **Example:** I dont know what to do. **don't**

16. Jatin couldnt help us take care of the cats. _____

17. He wont be able to come because he is ill. _____

18. Daniels new ballet classes will start in two weeks. _____

19. Thank you for hosting us all — its been a pleasure. _____

20. Theyre happy to discuss the changes to your plans. _____

21. The childrens toys broke when they fell off the table. _____

Section Two — Punctuation

Practice Questions

> Underline the option that uses hyphens correctly to complete each sentence. Look at this example:
>
> **Example:** The (top of-the-range   <u>top-of-the-range</u>) laptop broke.

22. Molly has a (**ten-year-old-snake   ten-year-old snake**) called Simon.

23. Lewis's (**accident-prone-sister   accident-prone sister**) tripped over a branch.

24. This (**state-of-the-art machine   state of the-art-machine**) will make our lives easier.

25. The scientists discovered a new species of (**cave dwelling-bats   cave-dwelling bats**).

26. The (**ever-more-exhausted man   ever-more exhausted man**) climbed the hill slowly.

27. The (**family-owned café   family owned café**) was established in 1975.

> Add the missing inverted commas and any other punctuation that is needed to complete each sentence. Look at this example:
>
> **Example:** " She would prefer this one , " claimed Steph.

28. I politely asked Could you lend me your red pencil, please

29. Lily said Thank you for cooking my dinner

30. Turn that music down now bellowed Anjali

31. She told me she wasn't coming replied Joey

32. Do you know what's happening over there Rob enquired.

Practice Questions

> Each sentence below is missing a colon or a semicolon. Circle the correct option from the brackets to complete each sentence. Look at this example:
>
> **Example:** Buy the following ingredients (**:** ;) flour, butter and eggs.

33. The carnival went down the street (: ;) the crowd was cheering wildly.

34. The kitchen was completely flooded (: ;) a water pipe had burst.

35. The acrobats performed their routine (: ;) the clowns waited in the wings.

36. These people need to see me (: ;) Hannah, Faisal and Luke.

37. This flight has been cancelled (: ;) ferries and train services are still running.

> Each of these sentences contains one punctuation error. Find and circle the error. Look at this example:
>
> **Example:** Would you like a cup of tea **!**

38. I was surprised when (quite suddenly) a mouse appeared).

39. Lionel declared. "This is the best play we've ever staged."

40. The town council would'nt listen to the residents' complaints.

41. I glued the vase back together: I hope they won't notice.

42. African elephants; which are the largest land mammals, live in herds.

43. If there's a problem with your computer, try looking at it's settings.

Section Two — Punctuation

Plurals

Plural means 'more than one'. So here's a plural number of pages about plurals. Enjoy...

Add 's' to make Most Words plural

Most plurals are formed by adding an 's':

mask ⟶ masks   Monday ⟶ Mondays

Other words have Different Rules

Words that End in 'ch', 'sh', 's', 'x' and 'z'

1) Put 'es' at the end of words ending in these letters.
2) You need to add the 'es' to make sure that you keep the soft sound in the original word.

kiss ⟶ kisses
watch ⟶ watches

Words that End in 'o'

1) Words that end in 'o' usually need 's' to make their plural, e.g. pianos, discos.
2) Some of these words are different though — they take 'es' instead. For example:

potatoes   tomatoes   heroes   echoes   dominoes

Words that End in 'f' and 'fe'

1) You need to add 'ves' to many words that end in 'f' and 'fe' to make them plural.

loaf ⟶ loaves   shelf ⟶ shelves   wife ⟶ wives

2) But again, some are different. These words just need an 's':

chiefs   chefs   beliefs   reefs   cliffs   riffs

Words that End in 'y'

1) If the letter before the 'y' is a vowel, just add 's' to make the plural:

toy ⟶ toys

2) If the letter before the 'y' is a consonant, the 'y' becomes 'ies' for the plural:

daisy ⟶ daisies

Vowels are the letters 'a', 'e', 'i', 'o' and 'u'. All the other letters of the alphabet are consonants.

Irregular Plurals

These words all change their vowel sound when they become plural:

| tooth ⟶ teeth | woman ⟶ women | mouse ⟶ mice |
| man ⟶ men | goose ⟶ geese | oasis ⟶ oases |

Section Three — Spelling

Plurals

You may be asked to Choose the Correct Plural

EXAMPLE: Circle the correct plural to complete each sentence below.

a) My family owns three *stereoes / stereoss / stereos / steroes*.
b) The clown at the circus was juggling with *knifes / kniffs / knifies / knives*.
c) My sister still believes in *faires / fairies / fairys / faireys*.
d) We have *mouses / mice / mise / mousies* living under the floorboards.

Method — Follow the rules for making plurals

1) Follow the <u>rules</u> to work out the <u>plurals</u>.
2) Remember to look out for any <u>exceptions</u> to the rules (see the previous page).

a) My family owns three *stereoes / stereoss /* (*stereos*) */ steroes*.

The word 'stereo' ends in 'o', so the plural ending has to be 's' or 'es'. → 'Stereo' takes the 's' ending — so the correct plural is 'stereos'.

b) The clown at the circus was juggling with *knifes / kniffs / knifies /* (*knives*).

'Knife' has an 'fe' ending. Many words ending in 'fe' take the plural 'ves', but some end in 's'. → The plural of 'knife' takes the more common 'ves' ending, so the answer is 'knives'.

c) My sister still believes in *faires /* (*fairies*) */ fairys / faireys*.

'Fairy' ends with a 'y', so you need to look at the letter before the 'y' to work out the correct plural ending. → The letter before the 'y' is a consonant — 'r'. So the plural of 'fairy' is 'fairies'.

d) We have *mouses /* (*mice*) */ mise / mousies* living under the floorboards.

The vowel sound of 'mouse' changes when it becomes plural. → The correct plural form of 'mouse' is 'mice'.

Practice Questions

1) Fill in the gap in each sentence, using the correct plural form of the word in brackets.

   a) We watched the monkey swing from the .... (branch) of the tree.
   b) I always brush my .... (tooth) twice a day.
   c) We're spending Christmas with the .... (Grady).   *This one is asking for the plural of a name.*
   d) Stefano is in the field picking .... (daisy).
   e) Would you like to try on any of those .... (dress)?

Revise the rules for forming plurals...

You might have to identify misspelt plurals in the test. You'll often be able to work out which words are wrong by following the rules for forming plurals, but make sure you know the exceptions too.

Section Three — Spelling

Homophones and Homographs

Don't be put off by these fancy words — they may sound a little bit complicated, but you probably know loads of homophones and homographs already without even realising.

Homophones sound the Same

1) Homophones are words that sound the same, but mean different things.
2) Here are lots of examples:

bean and been	root and route	weather and whether
pair and pear	rap and wrap	there, their and they're
wait and weight	blue and blew	by, buy and bye
maid and made	hire and higher	allowed and aloud

Homographs have the Same Spelling

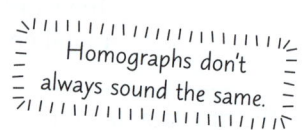

Homographs don't always sound the same.

1) Homographs are words that have the same spelling but a different meaning.
2) Here are some examples:

You need a bow and arrow to be an archer.

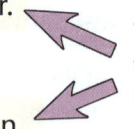

Remember that you must bow to the queen.

The word 'bow' has two different meanings in these sentences. You only know which meaning it is by reading the rest of the sentence.

The wind was howling round the house.

If you wind the handle it will play a tune.

The word 'wind' has different meanings, and it's pronounced differently in these two sentences.

A Pun is a Play on Words

Jokes that use homophones are called puns.

What do rabbits use to comb their fur? A hare brush.

Here 'hare' (an animal like a rabbit) is used instead of 'hair'. The two words are homophones.

I'm on a seafood diet — I see food and I eat it.

Seafood includes things like fish and prawns.

'See food' and 'seafood' are homophones.

Section Three — Spelling

Homophones and Homographs

You may be asked to **Select** the **Correct Homophone**

EXAMPLE: Circle the correct homophone to complete each sentence below.
   a) The supermarket is down by the *quay / key*.
   b) My arm was feeling very *saw / sore* when I woke up this morning.
   c) I can't *bear / bare* another day at school today.

Method — Look closely at the spelling of the homophones

1) Work out the meaning of the homophones in each sentence.
2) Then choose the correct homophone to fit the meaning of the sentence.

a) The supermarket is down by the (quay) / key.

A 'quay' is an area along a waterfront. It's somewhere that you may find a supermarket.
You open a lock using a 'key'. This meaning doesn't fit the sentence.

b) My arm was feeling very *saw* / (sore) when I woke up this morning.

'saw' could be the past tense of 'see' or a tool used for cutting wood.
'sore' means 'sensitive' and 'painful'. This is the correct answer — it fits in the sentence.

c) I can't (bear) / bare another day at school today.

'bear' is an animal, but it also means 'to endure' — this meaning fits the sentence.
'bare' means 'naked' or 'sparse'.

Be careful here — both 'bear' and 'saw' have several meanings. Don't let this confuse you.

Practice Questions

1) Circle the homophones that have been used incorrectly in the passage below.

> I'm supposed to go to drama group every Monday knight, but this weak I'm too tired. I've had a very busy day at school and I'm not feeling grate. Instead, I think I'm going to stay hear and watch a film that I haven't scene before.

2) Circle the correct homophone to complete each sentence below.
   a) Make sure that you know *wear / where* you are going.
   b) Watch out for the crab — it has very sharp *claws / clause*.
   c) At the theme park, we *road / rode* on four different roller coasters.
   d) The jockey pulled on the *reigns / reins* to get the horse to stop.

REVISION TIP

Practise putting homophones into sentences...

Using a clock or watch, give yourself three minutes to make a list of as many homophones as you can think of. Then try putting all the words you came up with into sentences.

Section Three — Spelling

Prefixes and Suffixes

Don't get your fixes in a twist. Prefixes and suffixes could come up in the test, so make sure you know how to use them and when suffixes change the spelling of the word they're added to.

Prefixes go at the Start of Words

Remember — 'pre' = 'before', so prefixes always go at the start of words.

1) Add a prefix at the start of a word to make a new word.
2) When you add a prefix, the spelling of the root word doesn't change.

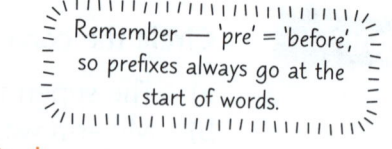

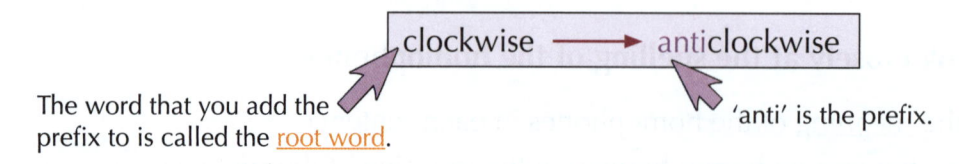

clockwise ⟶ anticlockwise

The word that you add the prefix to is called the root word.   'anti' is the prefix.

3) Here are some common prefixes and some examples of words that use each one:

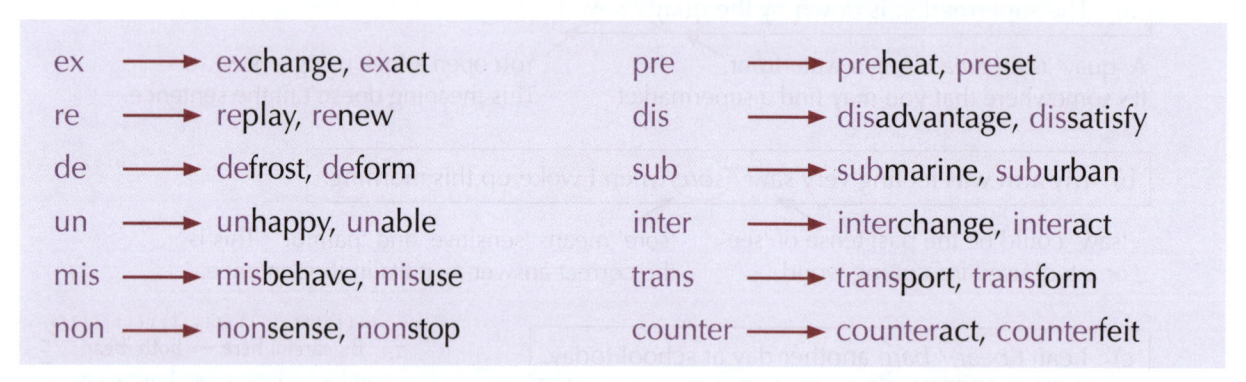

ex	⟶ exchange, exact		pre	⟶ preheat, preset
re	⟶ replay, renew		dis	⟶ disadvantage, dissatisfy
de	⟶ defrost, deform		sub	⟶ submarine, suburban
un	⟶ unhappy, unable		inter	⟶ interchange, interact
mis	⟶ misbehave, misuse		trans	⟶ transport, transform
non	⟶ nonsense, nonstop		counter	⟶ counteract, counterfeit

Suffixes go at the End of Words

1) Add a suffix to the end of a word to make a new word.

garden ⟶ gardener   turn ⟶ turning

'garden' is the root word.   'er' is the suffix.   'ing' is the suffix.

2) Here's a list of common suffixes with some words that use each one:

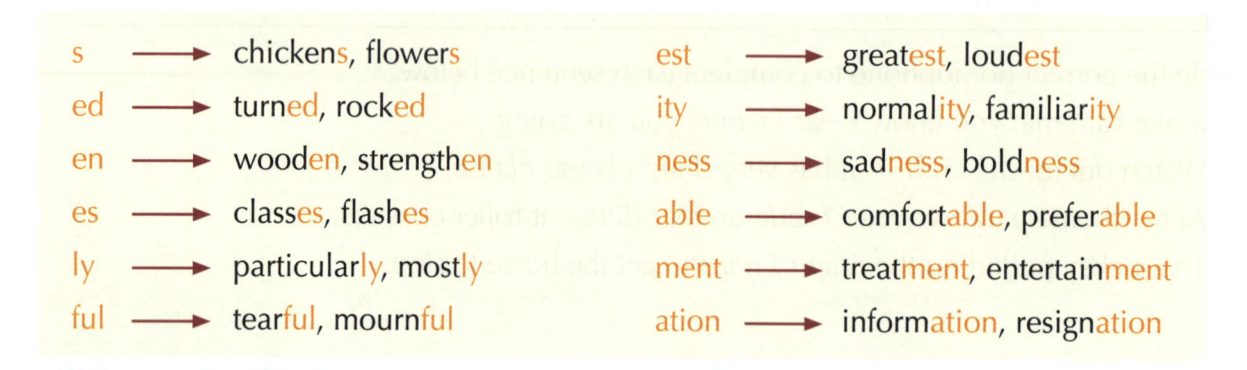

s	⟶ chickens, flowers		est	⟶ greatest, loudest
ed	⟶ turned, rocked		ity	⟶ normality, familiarity
en	⟶ wooden, strengthen		ness	⟶ sadness, boldness
es	⟶ classes, flashes		able	⟶ comfortable, preferable
ly	⟶ particularly, mostly		ment	⟶ treatment, entertainment
ful	⟶ tearful, mournful		ation	⟶ information, resignation

3) Remember that adding a suffix can sometimes change the spelling of the word:

travel ⟶ traveller   stop ⟶ stopping   take ⟶ taking

Section Three — Spelling

Prefixes and Suffixes

You could be asked to write the **Correct Prefix** or **Suffix**

EXAMPLE: Write the correct prefix or suffix to complete the words in the sentences.

    a) I asked the waiter for a ....fill of my soft drink.
    b) It was ....fortunate that you missed the last train home.
    c) The travell......... arrived an hour late after her flight was delayed.
    d) Angus is the tall......... boy in school.

Method — Read through each sentence carefully

1) You need to add a <u>prefix</u> to parts a) and b). Make sure that the prefix <u>agrees</u> with the meaning of the <u>rest</u> of the sentence.

> **a)** I asked the waiter for a **re**fill of my soft drink.

The speaker is asking for another drink.
The word is 'refill', so the correct prefix is 're'.

> **b)** It was **un**fortunate that you missed the last train home.

The sentence is talking about having bad luck,
so the correct prefix to add is 'un' to make 'unfortunate'.

2) Look at the <u>whole sentence</u> in parts c) and d) to help you choose the correct <u>suffix</u>.

> **c)** The travell**er** arrived an hour late after her flight was delayed.

You need to add a singular suffix here as the sentence talks about one person. Add 'er' to make 'traveller'.

'her' tells you that it was one person.

> **d)** Angus is the tall**est** boy in school.

You need to add 'est' to make 'tall' into a superlative.

Practice Questions

1) Complete the sentences by adding the correct prefix or suffix to the word in brackets.
    a) The baby polar bear is so _____ (adore).
    b) I was trying to be _____ (help) when I washed the dishes.
    c) The ball hit Kayley and knocked her _____ (conscious).
    d) Laszlo's feeling of _____ (happy) increased when he found his shoes.
    e) The apple was covered in mould and the flesh was _____ (rot).

The spelling of the root word may change.

TEST TIP — **Always check your spelling carefully...**
If you come across a word with a prefix or a suffix in the test, make sure that it's formed correctly — the examiners sometimes try to catch you out with tricky misspellings.

Section Three — Spelling

Silent Letters and Double Letters

Silent letters and double letters in words can trip up even the most accomplished spellers. There's a good chance that they'll come up in the test, so make sure you know them inside out...

Some words have **Silent Letters**

1) Some words are not spelt the way they sound. They have silent letters which you don't hear.
2) Here are some common examples:

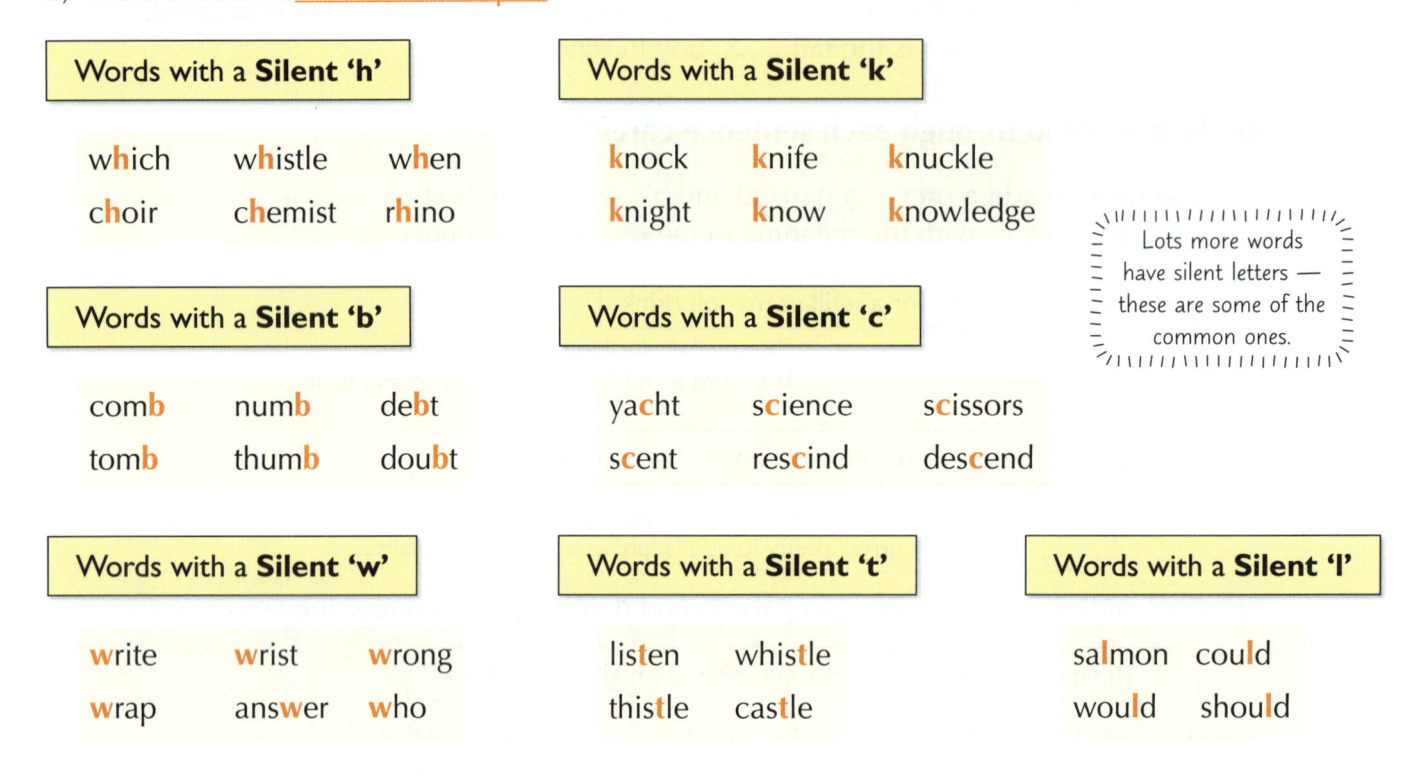

Words with a Silent 'h'
| which | whistle | when |
| choir | chemist | rhino |

Words with a Silent 'k'
| knock | knife | knuckle |
| knight | know | knowledge |

Words with a Silent 'b'
| comb | numb | debt |
| tomb | thumb | doubt |

Words with a Silent 'c'
| yacht | science | scissors |
| scent | rescind | descend |

Lots more words have silent letters — these are some of the common ones.

Words with a Silent 'w'
| write | wrist | wrong |
| wrap | answer | who |

Words with a Silent 't'
| listen | whistle |
| thistle | castle |

Words with a Silent 'l'
| salmon | could |
| would | should |

Words with **Double Letters** can be **Tricky**

These words have double letters that you say as a single sound:

accommodation	appalling
address	association
aggressive	balloon
annual	coffee

committed	disappear
deterrent	embarrass
different	essential
dilemma	eventually

exaggerate	jewellery
finally	necessary
immediately	occasion
irresistible	occurrence

parallel	spelling
possess	succeed
professor	success
recommend	tomorrow

Think of ways to remember spellings you find tricky, e.g. 'necessary' could be:
Never
Eat
Chips;
Eat
Salad
Sandwiches
And
Remain
Young.

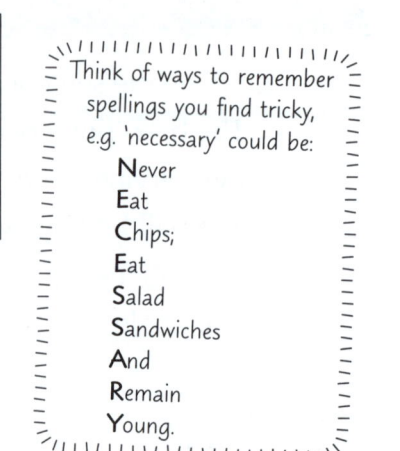

Section Three — Spelling

Silent Letters and Double Letters

You may have to find Words that are Spelt Wrong

EXAMPLE: Circle the spelling mistakes in the passage below.

> 1 Tomorow morning I leave for an autum trip with my youth group. We woud
> 2 like to go to the Lake District as we usually do, but instead we're going to the
> 3 New Forest. We've got lots of fun acttivities planned like hiking and climing,
> 4 and every knight we will sit by the campfire and eat toasted marshmallows.

Method — Look for silent letters and double letters

1) Work carefully through the passage <u>one line</u> at a time.
2) Look for words that are <u>missing</u> a silent letter, or where double letters are used <u>incorrectly</u>.

(Tomorrow) morning I leave for an (autumn) trip with my youth group. We (would)

'Tomorrow' has a double 'r'.   'autumn' has a silent 'n' at the end.   'would' has a silent 'l'.

like to go to the Lake District as we usually do, but instead we're going to the

There are no spelling mistakes in this line.

New Forest. We've got lots of fun (activities) planned like hiking and (climbing,)

A double 't' is not needed after 'c'. It should be spelt as 'activities'.   'climbing' has a silent 'b'.

and every (night) we will sit by the campfire and eat toasted marshmallows.

This should be 'night'. It isn't spelt with a silent 'k' when it means the opposite of day.

The context of the sentence should give you clues about how to spell some words.

Practice Questions

1) Each sentence contains one spelling mistake. Rewrite the sentences using the correct word.
   a) I maintainned a comfortable position for the whole journey.
   b) You need to wear more cloths in winter to keep warm.
   c) My interesting entry will win the competition tomorow.

2) Rewrite the sentences, using the correct word.
   a) Everyone agreed that the charity event had been *successful / successfull / sucessful*.
   b) While we're in London, we want to visit Nelson's *Colum / Collumn / Column*.
   c) Sasha is the most *intelligent / inteligent / inteliggent* girl in the class.
   d) I arrived just as the show was *begining / beginning / beggining*.

Practise spelling any words you find hard to remember...
Some of these words are pretty tricky, so write them out until they're firmly fixed in your noggin.

Section Three — Spelling

Other Awkward Spellings

Bad news, I'm afraid — some words are just plain tricky to spell. Some of them are pretty common too, so make sure you know how to spell them before you sit the test.

The 'i' before 'e' rule

1) Revise this rule — it's important:

   'i' before 'e' except after 'c', but only when it rhymes with bee.

   The whole word doesn't need to rhyme with bee, just the 'ie' sound.

2) Here are some examples:

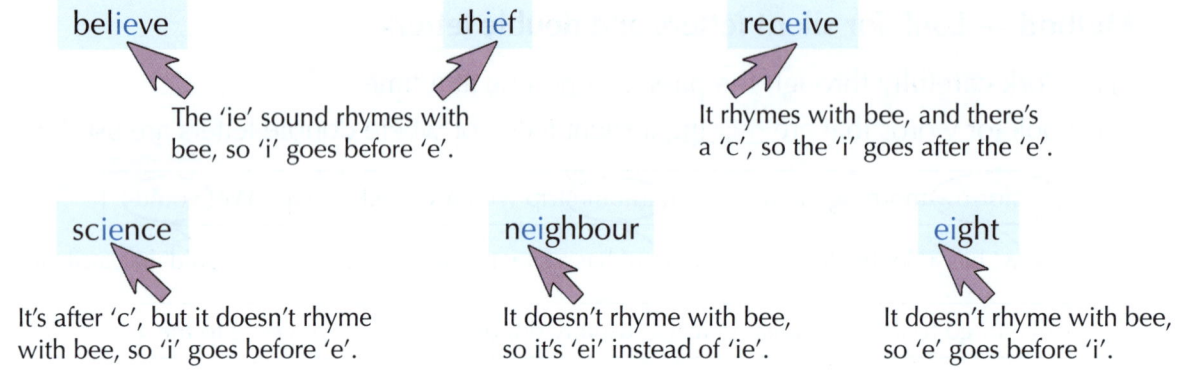

   believe — The 'ie' sound rhymes with bee, so 'i' goes before 'e'.

   thief

   receive — It rhymes with bee, and there's a 'c', so the 'i' goes after the 'e'.

   science — It's after 'c', but it doesn't rhyme with bee, so 'i' goes before 'e'.

   neighbour — It doesn't rhyme with bee, so it's 'ei' instead of 'ie'.

   eight — It doesn't rhyme with bee, so 'e' goes before 'i'.

3) There are a few exceptions to the rule, like 'weird' and 'seize'.

Unstressed Vowels can make words tricky to spell

1) Sometimes the vowel sound in a word isn't clear — these sounds are called unstressed vowels.

2) Spelling these words can be awkward because the vowels don't make the sound you would expect.

   Make up some short phrases to help you remember how to spell words with unstressed vowels, e.g. "I'm at a private party".

   private — 'private' sounds like it should be spelt 'privite'.

   separate — 'separate' sounds like it should be spelt 'seperate'.

3) Unfortunately there isn't a rule for spelling words with unstressed vowels — so make sure you know how to spell them. Here are some examples:

   definitely   doctor   occurrence
   ridiculous   difference   company
   government   animal   interference
   general   biscuit   carpet
   describe   jewellery   miserable

Section Three — Spelling

Other Awkward Spellings

> The exam may ask you to **Add Letters** to a **Word**

EXAMPLE: Choose either 'ie' or 'ei' to add to the sentences below.

a) Adam was rel___ved to find his maths homework.
b) There are p___ces of broken glass everywhere.
c) The villain was very dec___tful.
d) I often w___gh my cat to make sure that she is healthy.

Method — Remember the 'i before e' rule

1) Work out the word that is being added to each sentence.
2) Think carefully about the spelling — look at the letters before and after the gap.

a) Adam was relieved to find his maths homework.

The letter before the gap is 'l' and the 'ie' sound rhymes with bee. So 'ie' is the correct spelling to use.

b) There are pieces of broken glass everywhere.

The letter before the gap is 'p' and the 'ie' sound rhymes with bee. So 'pieces' should be spelt with an 'ie'.

Don't get confused by the 'c' after the gap — it doesn't matter which letter comes after the 'ie' sound.

c) The villain was very deceitful.

The letter before the gap is 'c' and the 'ie' sound rhymes with bee. This time you need to add 'ei' to spell 'deceitful'.

d) I often weigh my cat to make sure that she is healthy.

The letter before the gap is 'w', but the 'ie' sound does not rhyme with bee. You should add 'ei' to spell 'weigh'.

Practice Questions

1) Rewrite the sentences, using the correctly spelt word.
   a) My car is running out of *diesel / deisel*.
   b) Don't forget to paint the *cieling / ceiling*.
   c) Adaliz's *hieght / height* has increased by 9 cm this year.
   d) Mr Harris went to the museum to see the *ancient / anceint* remains.

2) The words below are missing unstressed vowels. Write the correct vowel in each gap.
   a) desp__rate
   b) fact__ry
   c) respons__ble
   d) harm__ny
   e) lit__r__ture
   f) pass__ge

Revise the exceptions to the 'i' before 'e' rule...

Spelling rules can come in handy during the test, but there are some words you just need to know...

Section Three — Spelling

Answering Spelling Questions

Here's a Multiple Choice question, or there's a Standard Answer one over the page — take your pick.

Multiple Choice — Finding the Spelling Mistakes

1) In a Multiple Choice test, you might be asked to find spelling mistakes in a passage of text.
2) The passage will be split into lines and each line will have either one mistake or no mistakes.
3) Here's an example:

EXAMPLE: There are some spelling errors in this passage. On each line there is either one mistake or no mistake at all. Find the group of words with the mistake in it and mark its letter on your answer sheet. If there is no mistake, mark N.

1 Children were apalled today after schools voted to ban lunchtime. The drastic
   A   B   C   D   N

2 measure has been implemented after politicians recieved reports that children
   A   B   C   D   N

3 were **h**aving too much fun. Children will know not be given breaks and one
   A   B   C   D   N

4 teacher beliefs that lunchtime should be filled with double history instead.
   A   B   C   D   N

Method — Read through each line carefully

1) You need to pick out the incorrectly spelt words. Look out for plural endings, silent letters, double letters and the 'i before e' rule as well as other misspelt words.
2) In the exam, you'd mark the letter for the group of words that includes the mistake on your answer sheet.

> 1 Children were **appalled** today after schools voted to ban lunchtime. The drastic

'appalled' is spelt with a double 'p'. This is the error in this line, so the answer is B.

> 2 measure has been implemented after politicians **received** reports that children

The 'ie' sound rhymes with bee, and it directly follows a 'c'. So it should be spelt 'received' and the answer is C.

> 3 were having too much fun. Children will **now** not be given breaks and one

The word 'now' does not have a silent 'k', so the answer is C.

> 4 teacher **believes** that lunchtime should be filled with double history instead.

'beliefs' is a plural noun — the correct verb form is 'believes', which means the answer is A.

Section Three — Spelling

Answering Spelling Questions

Standard Answer — Correcting Spelling Mistakes

1) On the Standard Answer paper you may be given a passage containing spelling errors.
2) You could be asked to rewrite the passage, using the correct spellings. Here's an example:

EXAMPLE:

The passage below contains some spelling errors.
Rewrite the passage, correcting the spelling mistakes.

> Janet was certain that she had mannaged to grow the largest pumpkin this year. She had bean growing the pumpkin for eleven months and it now wieghed over 50 kilograms. She new that the competition would be fierce though; there were usualy at least 20 entrys. Moreover, Janet had no idea how she was going to transport the pumpkin to the awards cerremony witch was taking place the very next day.
>
> *(8 marks)*

Method — Read the passage carefully

1) Read through the passage at least twice, underlining words that are spelt incorrectly.
2) Next, write down the spellings that you should use instead beside each incorrect word.
3) Rewrite the passage, replacing the incorrectly spelt words with the correct spellings. Check that the passage makes sense and you haven't changed words that were correct.

> Janet was certain that she had **managed** to grow the largest pumpkin this year.

There is only one 'n' in 'managed'.

> She had **been** growing the pumpkin for eleven months and it now **weighed** over

'Bean' and 'been' are homophones. 'been' should be used here.

The 'ie' sound does not rhyme with bee, so it should be spelt 'weighed'.

> 50 kilograms. She **knew** that the competition would be fierce though; there were

The verb 'knew' has a silent 'k' which should be added here.

> **usually** at least 20 **entries**. Moreover, Janet had no idea how she was going to transport

'usually' has a double 'l'.

The plural of 'entry' is spelt 'entries'.

Remember the rule — if the letter before 'y' is a consonant, add 'ies' for the plural endings.

> the pumpkin to the awards **ceremony which** was taking place the very next day.

'ceremony' is spelt with a single 'r'.

'Witch' and 'which' are homophones. 'which' is the correct version to use here.

TEST TIP

Don't just skim-read the text — go through it carefully...

Some of the mistakes in the passage may be quite tricky to pick up. If you don't spot any errors in a line right away, make sure you really **look** at and **think** about each word.

Section Three — Spelling

Practice Questions

In the test, you may well be asked to spell some tricky words. Have a go at these practice questions to see how well you know the rules and if there are any topics you need to revise again.

Write the correct plural of the word in the brackets. Look at this example:

Example: The shop had sold out of ___scarves___ (scarf).

1. The _____ had forgotten that they had a swimming lesson today. **(boy)**

2. All of the _____ around our house are full of wildlife. **(marsh)**

3. Several _____ wanted to host the Olympic Games. **(city)**

4. Both _____ of the pizza were delicious. **(half)**

5. I don't have enough general knowledge to win many _____. **(quiz)**

Underline the correct homophone to complete the sentence. Look at this example:

Example: I had to (ring <u>wring</u>) out my wet clothes.

6. A lot of (**waste waist**) ends up in landfill rather than being recycled.

7. Helena bought some (**leaks leeks**) to have with dinner.

8. Eva told an exciting (**storey story**) about her adventure in outer space.

9. Several (**panes pains**) of glass had been smashed by debris during the storm.

10. The ball was (**throne thrown**) back over the fence by the friendly neighbour.

11. The farmers (**sow sew**) the fields with wheat and barley.

Section Three — Spelling

Practice Questions

> Add the correct prefix or suffix to each word to complete the sentences. Look at this example:
>
> **Example:** Libby's birthday was a delight __ful__ occasion.

12. We apologised wholeheartedly for the _____understanding.

13. Everything they said about me was entire_____ false.

14. Malik finds his employ_____ in a supermarket very fulfilling.

15. A large van _____ports vegetables from our farm to a local restaurant.

16. All of the lights in our house stopped working, so we called an electri_____.

17. Gemma found Alfie's behaviour completely _____acceptable.

> In each sentence, one word with a silent letter has been spelt incorrectly. Underline the word and write the correct spelling on the line. Look at this example:
>
> **Example:** I think it woud be a good idea. __would__

18. Billy made a delicious rubarb crumble. _____

19. Lydia has an extensive nowledge of local history. _____

20. The pluming in the old house needed a complete overhaul. _____

21. The enormous cat riggled out from beneath the mauve sofa. _____

22. The marathon runner was very disiplined — he trained every day. _____

Section Three — Spelling

Practice Questions

> Each sentence contains one error in the use of double letters. Underline the word with the error and write the correct spelling on the line. Look at this example:
>
> **Example:** We signed in each <u>atendee</u> one at a time.   _attendee_

23. We asessed the merits and pitfalls of the plan. _____

24. The artist had drawn fabulous ilustrations for the novel. _____

25. The children colected petals from different flowers. _____

26. We returned the uneeded cutlery to the cabinet. _____

27. Some pigs have an apetite for truffles, so they rummage for them. _____

> Underline the correct spelling of the word in the brackets to complete each sentence. Look at this example:
>
> **Example:** I can't find the (reciept   <u>receipt</u>) anywhere.

28. Tina has painted the walls an awful shade of (**beige   biege**).

29. Grandad says he used to get up to all sorts of (**mischief   mischeif**) at school.

30. The lorries carried their heavy (**freight   frieght**) onto the ferry.

31. Martin swaggered over with a (**concieted   conceited**) smile on his face.

32. They heard a high-pitched (**shreik   shriek**) from the other room.

33. The knight (**wielded   weilded**) the sword with great skill.

Section Three — Spelling

Practice Questions

> Write the correct vowel in each gap below to complete the words. Look at this example:
>
> **Example:** It is gener_a_lly best to avoid that topic.

34. Every Saturday, George went to the libr___ry to borrow a new book.

35. Annabel was extremely int___rested in archaeology.

36. I had to do the washing-up all week as a punishm___nt.

37. Cara's office had to hire a new secr___t___ry after Kevin retired.

38. Attending the school fair was vol___nt___ry, but everyone in Ola's class was going.

> Each sentence contains one spelling mistake. Underline the incorrectly spelt word and write the correct spelling on the line. Look at this example:
>
> **Example:** I was <u>sheilded</u> from view by a tree. ____shielded____

39. The soldiers stood defiently before the opposing battalion. _____

40. Mel requested that the publishers didn't altar any spellings. _____

41. We jogged along an indistinct footpath that ran paralel to the river. _____

42. Jane was ingrossed in a lengthy biography — it had two volumes. _____

43. The professional jewel thieves scemed together before the heist. _____

44. Milo found Cleo's allegations to be entirely implausable. _____

Section Three — Spelling

Section Four — Writers' Techniques

Alliteration and Onomatopoeia

English is full of long words for really simple things — here are two of them...

Alliteration is the repetition of Consonant Sounds

1) Alliteration is the repetition of a sound at the beginning of nearby words.
2) It emphasises certain words and makes a sentence more memorable.

Sally slipped on a slimy slug.

Alliteration usually occurs with consonants.

There are lots of 's' and 'sl' sounds in this sentence.

The dirty dog drooled all over the doormat.

In this sentence, the 'd' sound is repeated.

Onomatopoeia is when a word Sounds like the Noise it Describes

1) Onomatopoeic words sound like the noise they describe.
2) Here are some examples:

| fizz | bang | crash | crunch | splash | plop | drip |

You may be asked to identify Onomatopoeic words in a Passage

EXAMPLE: Circle the onomatopoeic words in the passage below.

> Amy signalled to Kofi and they sneaked into the garage. The ladder scraped across the floor as they tried to move it. They carried the ladder and put it up against the tree. As soon as they did, Tiddles miaowed happily and pattered safely down.

Method — Look for words that describe noises

1) Read through the passage looking for words that sound like the noise they're describing.
2) If you're not sure about a word, say it to yourself. Listen carefully to the sound it makes.

Amy signalled to Kofi and they sneaked into the garage. The ladder (scraped) across

These words aren't onomatopoeic — they don't sound like a noise.

'scraped' is onomatopoeic — it sounds like the noise it is describing.

the floor as they tried to move it. They carried the ladder and put it up against

There are no onomatopoeic words in this line.

the tree. As soon as they did, Tiddles (miaowed) happily and (pattered) safely down.

'miaowed' sounds like the noise a cat makes — this is onomatopoeic.

'pattered' is also onomatopoeic.

Section Four — Writers' Techniques

Alliteration and Onomatopoeia

Make sure that you can spot **Alliteration** in a **Sentence**

EXAMPLE: Circle the letters that alliterate in these sentences.
a) Michael's scary school project scooped first prize.
b) The king kept kicking the kind knight.
c) She surely made the sugar shapes.
d) Felicity photographed forests for her family.

Method — Find the sound that's repeated in the sentence

1) You have to circle the sounds that are repeated.
2) Listen to the sound made by the letters at the beginning of each word in the sentence.

a) Michael's (scary) (school) project (scooped) first prize.
   The 'sc' sound alliterates in this sentence.

Remember that alliteration is the repetition of the same sound rather than the same letter.

b) The (king) (kept) (kicking) the (kind) knight.

This sentence has a repeated 'k' sound. Although 'knight' begins with a 'k', this letter is silent so it doesn't alliterate with the other words. The 'k' in the middle of 'kicking' doesn't alliterate because it's in the middle of the word.

c) She (surely) made the (sugar) (shapes).
   The 'sh' sound alliterates in this sentence.

d) (Felicity) (photographed) (forests) (for) her (family).
   In this sentence it's the 'f' sound that is repeated — even though 'photographed' is spelt with a 'ph', it's still pronounced with an 'f'.

Practice Questions

1) Say whether each sentence is an example of onomatopoeia, alliteration or neither.
   a) Cosima circled the church.
   b) The door banged in the wind.
   c) Studying psychology suits Susan.
   d) He shouted loudly as the train sped past.
   e) Whose work is wrong?
   f) The chickens clucked in the yard.

TEST TIP **Try saying the sentences in your head...**
Onomatopoeia and alliteration are all about the sounds that words make. Imagine reading the sentences out loud and think about how different sounds are used.

Section Four — Writers' Techniques

Imagery

Imagery is another word for descriptive writing — it's often used in fiction texts.

Figurative Language gives you a Picture

1) Literal language means exactly what it says.

   > Dave is a real clown.

   If you are talking about someone called Dave who works as a clown, then this is a literal statement.

2) Figurative language doesn't mean exactly what it says.

   > Dave is a real clown.

   If you're describing someone who jokes around a lot but who isn't actually a clown, then this is a figurative statement.

3) Imagery is a type of figurative language — it's language that is used to give the reader a vivid picture of something.

   > The field of tulips I saw from the window was like a red carpet stretching into the distance.

   This imagery makes you imagine a red carpet in your mind, and this shows you what the field of tulips was like.

   > The pie smelt like feet, and its crust was concrete.

   This imagery helps you to imagine what the pie smelt like...

   ... and this imagery tells you how hard the crust was, but you know it isn't actually made of concrete.

There are lots of different types of Imagery

A Simile says that One Thing is Like Another

1) A simile describes something by comparing it to something else.
2) Similes always use a comparing word like 'as' or 'like'.

   > His anger erupted like a volcano.

   The simile helps you to imagine the force of his anger.

   > Anja's cheeks were as white as snow.

   This simile emphasises how white Anja's cheeks were.

   > Life is like a rollercoaster.

   Life is being compared to a rollercoaster in this simile.

Section Four — Writers' Techniques

Imagery

A **Metaphor** says that **One Thing Is Another**

1) A metaphor describes something as actually being something else.
2) It's an example of figurative writing.

> Vittorio's eyes were deep black oily pools.

This gives a vivid description of Vittorio's eyes, but they're not actually deep black oily pools.

> The living room was a furnace.

The living room wasn't actually a furnace, but the metaphor shows that the room was very hot.

Analogies are like **Extended Similes**

1) An analogy is a comparison between two similar things.
2) It compares two different things to help explain something to the reader.

> The rainforest is being cut down at an incredible speed. An area of rainforest equal to twenty football pitches is lost every minute.

This part is the analogy. It helps you to visualise exactly how quickly the rainforest is being cut down.

> She was hoping to pass the test without studying at all, which is like hoping to win the lottery without buying a ticket.

This helps you understand how unlikely something is by comparing it to an impossible situation.

Personification describes a **Thing** as a **Person**

Personification describes something that's not human as if it is a person.

Personification makes descriptions come to life.

> The sea races up the beach.

This sounds like the sea has the ability to run.

> The sun smiled on the shoppers below.

This sounds like the sun has a human expression.

> Time had been kind to Raj; there was not a wrinkle on his face.

This sounds like time was deliberately nice to Raj.

Make sure you know the difference between similes and metaphors...

Similes and metaphors can be pretty confusing. Remember, if a sentence **compares** something to something else, then it's a simile. If it says that something **is** something else, then it's a metaphor.

Section Four — Writers' Techniques

Imagery

You may have to Recognise Different Types of Imagery

EXAMPLE: Read the passage below. Then answer the questions that follow.

> It was the hottest day of summer. The sun was a golden lamp in the sky, casting rays onto the sunbathers who were lying on the sand. Cries of excitement from the seagulls competed for attention with the shouts of ice cream sellers strolling along the beach. Like a swan crossing a lake, a boat cruised slowly past in the distance.

a) Find one example of a simile in the passage.
b) Give one example of personification in the passage.
c) Give one example of a metaphor from the passage.

Method — Look closely for different types of imagery

1) Read through the whole passage. Start to look for the different types of imagery.
2) For part a) you need to find a simile. Look for comparisons using 'like' or 'as ... as'.

   Like a swan crossing a lake, a boat cruised slowly past in the distance.

   The boat in the distance is compared to a swan crossing a lake. This is a simile.

3) Part b) asks you to find an example of personification. You need to find a point in the passage where something is given human qualities.

   Cries of excitement from the seagulls competed for attention

   Saying that the seagulls cried out with "excitement" gives them a human quality, so it's an example of personification.

4) To find a metaphor for part c), look for something being described as something else.

   The sun was a golden lamp in the sky,

   The sun is described as being 'a golden lamp' — it's a metaphor.

You could use imagery to make your writing more interesting — have a look at p.97 for more.

Practice Questions

1) Write down whether each sentence is a simile, a metaphor, or personification.
   a) Luck had not been kind to Karl — his trousers had ripped in two.
   b) Fatima's clothes were as heavy as a coat of armour.
   c) The cold hand of fear gripped Luke's heart.
   d) The packed classroom was as silent as a library.
   e) Gary's fingers were icicles when he'd finished playing volleyball in the snow.

TEST TIP — **Don't rush when answering imagery questions...**

It's easy to make mistakes with imagery questions. Before you answer a question, think very carefully about what is being described and what kind of imagery is being used.

Section Four — Writers' Techniques

Abbreviations

You see acronyms and initialisms everywhere. Make sure you know the difference between them.

Abbreviations are Shortened Words

1) Abbreviations are shortened versions of words, for example:

bicycle → bike   refrigerator → fridge   hippopotamus → hippo

2) Longer phrases can be shortened in two main ways:

Initialisms are Said as Letters

Initialisms use the first letters of words in a phrase — they are pronounced as separate letters.

PC = personal computer   UN = United Nations   PTO = please turn over

Acronyms are Said as Words

Acronyms usually use the first letters of words in a phrase to make a new word.

NATO = North Atlantic Treaty Organisation

Sometimes more than one letter from each word is used to form the acronym.

Radar = radio detection and ranging   ← The 'ra' at the start of radio make up the first two letters of 'radar'.

Practice Questions

1) Give the abbreviated version of each of these words.
   a) rhinoceros   b) electronic mail   c) influenza

2) Give the full word for these abbreviations.
   a) dino   b) telly   c) lab

3) Write down whether each word below is an abbreviation, an initialism or an acronym.
   a) CD   b) approx.   c) NASA   d) DVD   e) BBC

REVISION TIP — **Look out for abbreviations in books and newspapers...**
When you spot an initialism or an acronym somewhere, try to find out what it stands for. You never know — an abbreviation you look up might just pop up in your test.

Section Four — Writers' Techniques

Irony and Rhetorical Questions

Two more techniques for you to revise here. In the test, you could be asked to identify when a writer has used irony or rhetorical questions, so make sure you can spot them from twenty paces.

Irony is often used to Create Humour

Verbal Irony is where the Opposite Meaning is meant

1) Verbal irony is where the writer means the opposite to what they have actually written.
2) You can usually tell that the writer is being ironic from the context of the writing.

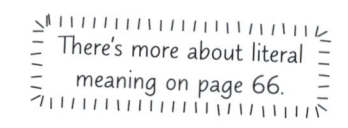

There's more about literal meaning on page 66.

> We were stranded at the airport for 48 hours with no food, which was just great.

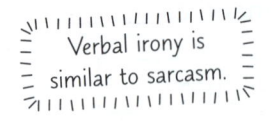

Verbal irony is similar to sarcasm.

The writer doesn't actually mean that it was great — they actually mean the opposite. This is irony.

Situational Irony is where Unexpected Events Occur

Situational irony is where the opposite thing happens to what the reader expects.

> While the two robbers were robbing the bank, someone stole their car.

We don't expect someone to steal from the robbers. This is an example of situational irony — it is the opposite of what we expect to happen.

A Rhetorical Question Isn't a Proper Question

1) A rhetorical question is a question that you are not expected to answer.
2) They are often designed to make you think, or to make you do something.
3) Rhetorical questions are often used in texts that are trying to persuade the reader, such as newspaper articles or adverts.

> When will the world take notice of what is going on?

This a rhetorical question — no one knows the answer. It is designed to make you think about what is happening.

> How many times have I told you not to run in the corridor?

You're not meant to answer this question. The speaker is reminding you that you should not run in the corridor.

Section Four — Writers' Techniques

Irony and Rhetorical Questions

You may be asked to spot **Irony** and **Rhetorical Questions**

EXAMPLE: Read the passage below. Then answer the questions that follow.

> "Have you ever heard such a ridiculous excuse?" asked Mrs Hunter when Mildred told her that her homework had blown away. "It's even worse because you forgot your homework last week as well, didn't you?" Mildred admitted that she had indeed forgotten her homework the previous week, but this hadn't been her fault either, as her computer had broken. "Of course, none of this matters," continued Mrs Hunter. "It's not as if doing your homework will help you to pass your exams."

a) Find one example of irony in the passage.
b) Give one example of a rhetorical question in the passage.

Method — Look for irony and unanswered questions

1) You need to find an example of irony in the passage for part a). Remember that this can be found when someone is speaking.

   "It's not as if doing your homework will help you to pass your exams."

   This is verbal irony — Mrs Hunter means the opposite. Doing her homework will help Mildred to pass her exams.

2) For part b) you need to find a rhetorical question — look for an unanswered question in the passage.

   "Have you ever heard such a ridiculous excuse?"

   Mildred answers the other question that Mrs Hunter asks her — she admits that she had forgotten her homework the week before.

   This is a rhetorical question. You can tell this because Mrs Hunter doesn't expect Mildred to answer it, and so she continues to speak.

Practice Questions

1) Read the following sentences. Put a tick next to the ones that show irony.
   a) I play hockey on Saturdays whether it rains or not.
   b) Ed had saved up all year for his new toy, only to be given it for Christmas.
   c) I went to the shop to buy gravy granules and they were on special offer.
   d) Maggie stepped around a puddle and ended up falling into a pond.
   e) I'm allergic to apples, but my brother is allergic to pears.

Don't you just love rhetorical questions?

If there isn't an answer to a question in a text, chances are it's a rhetorical question. Irony can sometimes be a bit trickier to spot, but it's often found when a writer is being humorous.

Section Four — Writers' Techniques

Idioms, Clichés and Proverbs

Idioms, clichés and proverbs are different types of phrases — you hear them all the time.

Idioms are Phrases that Aren't Meant Literally

Literal language means exactly what it says (see p.66).

1) Idioms are common phrases that most people use and understand.
2) They have a meaning that is different to the literal meaning of the words.
3) You can only understand an idiom if you know what it means.

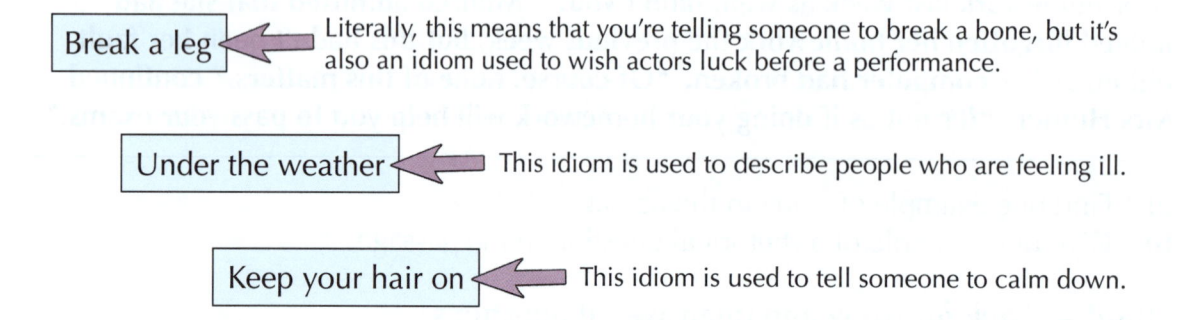

> Break a leg ← Literally, this means that you're telling someone to break a bone, but it's also an idiom used to wish actors luck before a performance.

> Under the weather ← This idiom is used to describe people who are feeling ill.

> Keep your hair on ← This idiom is used to tell someone to calm down.

Clichés are Overused Phrases

1) A cliché is a phrase that has been overused and has lost some of its impact.
2) Clichés are often metaphors (see page 67).

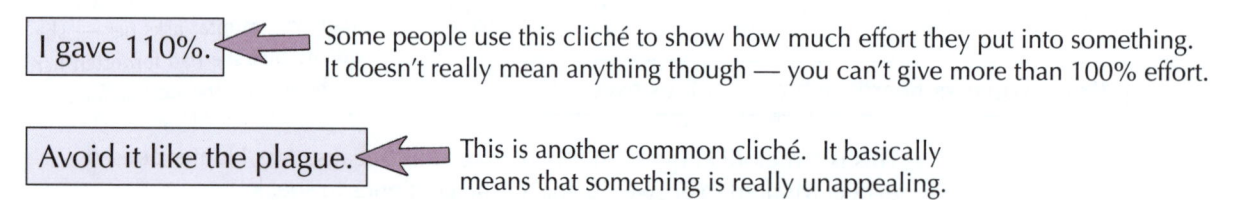

Try not to use clichés in your writing — they're really unoriginal.

> I gave 110%. ← Some people use this cliché to show how much effort they put into something. It doesn't really mean anything though — you can't give more than 100% effort.

> Avoid it like the plague. ← This is another common cliché. It basically means that something is really unappealing.

3) Many idioms are also clichés because they're common phrases that people use a lot.

Proverbs are Phrases that Give Advice

1) Proverbs are short phrases that are commonly used.
2) They usually give a general truth or words of advice for how to do something.

> Too many cooks spoil the broth.

This means that it's a bad idea to have too many people doing the same thing.

> Don't judge a book by its cover.

This proverb means that you shouldn't judge people or objects by the way they look.

Section Four — Writers' Techniques

Idioms, Clichés and Proverbs

Make sure that you can recognise Idioms, Clichés and Proverbs

EXAMPLE: Each sentence below contains either an idiom or a proverb. Write down which type is used in each sentence.

a) My brother is really winding me up today.
b) Ben's got a chip on his shoulder.
c) Look after the pennies and the pounds will look after themselves.

Method — Think about each sentence's meaning

Identify the phrase in each sentence and think about whether it's an idiom or a proverb.

Take a look back at the previous page if you're not sure about the difference.

a) My brother is really **winding me up** today.

'winding me up' is a common phrase. The person isn't actually being wound up though — it means that they're being annoyed. This is an idiom.

b) Ben's got a **chip on his shoulder**.

This sentence means Ben's angry about something — he doesn't literally have a chip on his shoulder. This sentence isn't giving advice, so it's an idiom.

c) **Look after the pennies and the pounds will look after themselves.**

This whole sentence is a proverb — it means that if you save small amounts, it'll add up to bigger savings.

Practice Questions

1) Write out the meaning of each of the following:
   a) You're going to end up in hot water if you carry on like this.
   b) I put blood, sweat and tears into my maths homework.
   c) It's time to throw in the towel.
   d) I wish the politician would stop beating about the bush.
   e) My little brother is really driving me up the wall.

TEST TIP

Pull your socks up and revise idioms, clichés and proverbs...

If you need to identify a proverb or idiom, think about what the phrase is doing. If it's giving advice, it's a proverb, but if it's more like a common phrase, it's probably an idiom.

Section Four — Writers' Techniques

Synoynms and Antonyms

You've almost covered all the tricky words, here are the last two — synonym and antonym.

Synonyms are words that Mean the Same

1) Words that can mean the same thing are synonyms.
2) Here are a few examples of synonyms:

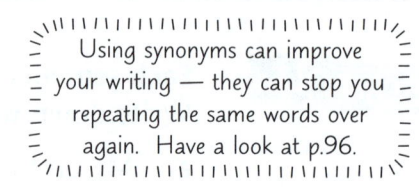

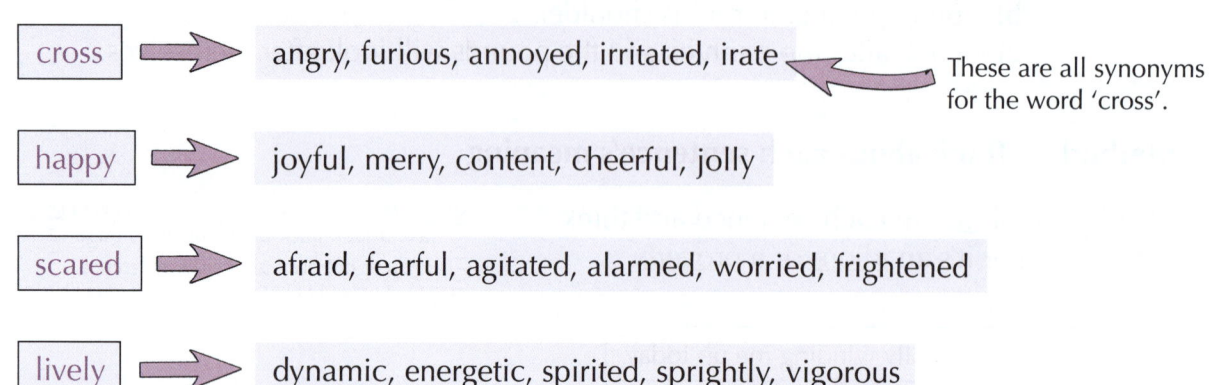

| cross ➡ | angry, furious, annoyed, irritated, irate |

These are all synonyms for the word 'cross'.

| happy ➡ | joyful, merry, content, cheerful, jolly |

| scared ➡ | afraid, fearful, agitated, alarmed, worried, frightened |

| lively ➡ | dynamic, energetic, spirited, sprightly, vigorous |

Using synonyms can improve your writing — they can stop you repeating the same words over again. Have a look at p.96.

Antonyms are words that Mean the Opposite

1) Antonyms are words like 'hot' and 'cold' — they are opposites.
2) These are examples of antonyms:

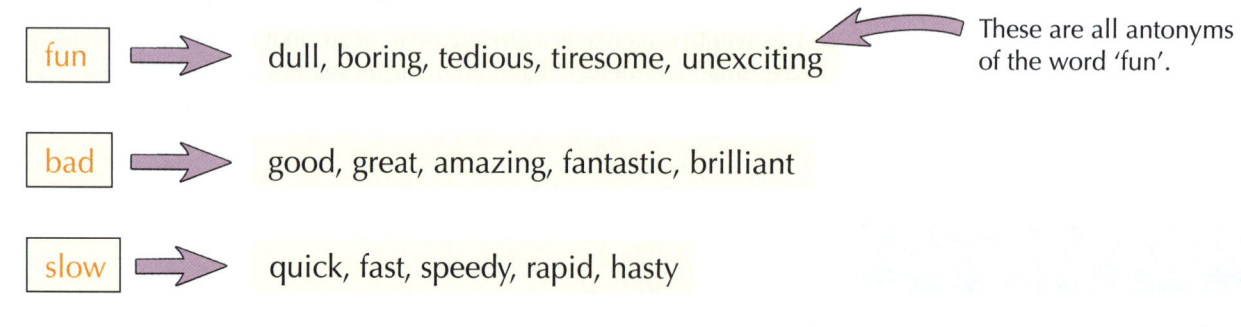

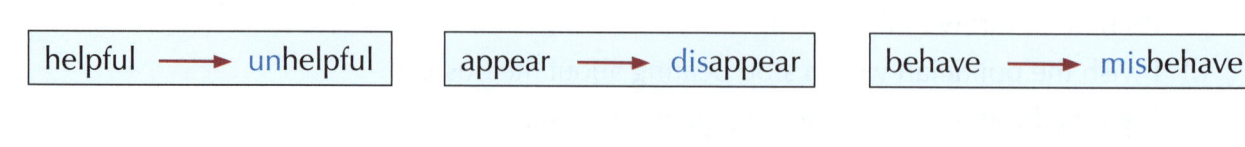

| fun ➡ | dull, boring, tedious, tiresome, unexciting |

These are all antonyms of the word 'fun'.

| bad ➡ | good, great, amazing, fantastic, brilliant |

| slow ➡ | quick, fast, speedy, rapid, hasty |

Antonyms can be made by adding a Prefix to a Root Word...

helpful ⟶ unhelpful   appear ⟶ disappear   behave ⟶ misbehave

There's more about prefixes and suffixes on page 52.

... or by changing a Suffix

careful ⟶ careless   painful ⟶ painless   tactful ⟶ tactless

Section Four — Writers' Techniques

Synoynms and Antonyms

You may be asked to find Synonyms and Antonyms of Words

EXAMPLE: Read the passage and then answer the questions that follow.

> The owl sat upon the bridge feeling disgruntled, staring down at her reflection in the water below. Only that morning she had been the wisest owl in the forest, but that accolade had been taken by her ecstatic sister. Her eyes suddenly focused on the pool below as a small face broke the surface.

a) Pick a word from the passage that means the same as 'annoyed'.
b) Pick a word from the passage that means the opposite of 'miserable'.

Method — Think carefully about what each word means

1) Work out the meaning of the word in the question, then read the text again.
2) If you don't know what the word in the question means, look for clues in the passage.
3) Part a) asks you to find a word that means the same as 'annoyed':

> The owl sat upon the bridge feeling disgruntled...

'disgruntled' has the same meaning as 'annoyed', so that's the answer.

Look at the passage to help you. The owl is upset because she's no longer the wisest, so you can guess that 'disgruntled' means 'annoyed'.

4) For part b), you need to find the opposite of 'miserable':

> ...but that accolade had been taken by her ecstatic sister.

'ecstatic' means very happy, so it has the opposite meaning to 'miserable'.

Her sister has just become the wisest owl, so if you're not sure, you can guess that 'ecstatic' means happy.

Practice Questions

1) Circle the correct synonym for the word in bold.
   a) Losing my job left me feeling **desolate** (*hopeless / disappointed / furious*).
   b) The dark clouds overhead were **ominous** (*drifting / threatening / depressing*).
   c) The boy walked to his lesson **briskly** (*indifferently / hurriedly / precisely*).

2) Circle the correct antonym for the word in bold.
   a) Max shouted at her in a **patronising** way (*helpful / respectful / cheeky*).
   b) The news left my grandparents **jubilant** (*overjoyed / concerned / despondent*).
   c) The assembly was very **tedious** (*arduous / stimulating / boring*).

Don't confuse synonyms and antonyms...

You can remember which one's which by remembering that **s**ynonyms have the **s**ame meaning as each other. And then that means that antonyms must have the opposite meaning to each other.

Section Four — Writers' Techniques

Answering Word Type Questions

There's nothing like a couple of sample questions to help you get ready for the exam...

Multiple Choice — Identifying Word Types

1) In the test, you might be asked questions about the <u>word types</u> a writer has used.
2) You'll be asked to <u>read</u> a passage and then answer some <u>questions</u> about <u>what you've read</u>.
3) Here's an example of the sort of thing you might see in the test:

> **EXAMPLE:** Read the poem below and then answer the following questions.
>
> **An adapted extract from *A Mother to Her Waking Infant* by Joanna Baillie**
>
> 1 When sudden wakes the sullen shriek,
>   And redder swells thy little cheek;
>   When jingled keys thy woe beguile,
>   And thro' the wet eye gleams the smile,
> 5 Still for thy weakly self is spent
>   Thy little silly complaint.
>
> *This is just an extract — the text in the test will usually be longer than this.*
>
> 1) What is 'sudden wakes the sullen shriek' (line 1) an example of?
>   A Rhetorical Question   D A metaphor
>   B Personification   E Irony
>   C Alliteration
>
> 2) What is 'jingled' (line 3) an example of?
>   A Alliteration   D A simile
>   B Personification   E Situational irony
>   C Onomatopoeia
>
> **Method — Read the examples in the question carefully**
>
> *Look at the context of the passage to help you work out the techniques that the author has used.*
>
> 1) Think about the <u>techniques</u> mentioned in each question. Look at the <u>line reference</u> to find the quote in the poem.
> 2) Read the <u>quote</u> in question 1. Look for <u>patterns</u> in the <u>word sounds</u> and think about whether the meaning is <u>literal</u> or <u>figurative</u>.
>
> When **s**udden wakes the **s**ullen **s**hriek ← The poet has repeated the 's' sound — this is an example of alliteration.
>
> 3) You can work out the answer to question 2 by thinking about <u>what the word sounds like</u>.
>
> jingled ← 'jingled' sounds like keys being shaken, so it's an example of onomatopoeia.
>
> *Look at the remaining options to check that you've chosen the correct technique.*

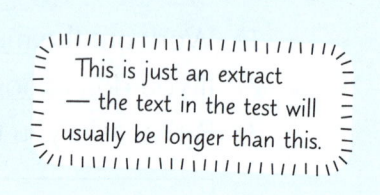

Section Four — Writers' Techniques

Answering Word Type Questions

Standard Answer — Finding Word Types in a passage

EXAMPLE: Read the passage below and then answer the questions that follow.

> **Selworth — worth visiting?**
>
> 1   Wide sandy beaches. Picturesque vistas. These are just some of the things that you won't witness if you choose to spend your holiday this year in Selworth. Instead, you can expect to hear the constant whine of traffic, the clanging of heavy machinery and the ferocious shouts of the locals going about their daily lives.
>
> 5   Of course, there is still the famous Selworth Castle. Sadly, the 'insightful and historical day out' offered by the guidebook is not granted by the steep admission prices and the sheer overcrowding. I was like a rush-hour commuter on the Underground trying to move between rooms; I decided to call it a day after 45 minutes and go for a bowl of soup in the restaurant, but it was cold.

a) The word 'clanging' (line 3) is an example of which technique?

b) 'I was like a rush-hour commuter on the Underground' (lines 7-8). Which type of imagery is used here?

c) Find an example of an idiom in the passage.

Method — Think carefully about the different word types

1) Part a) asks you to name the technique that is used in the word 'clanging':

   ...the clanging of heavy machinery...

   The word 'clanging' sounds like the noise it makes. So 'clanging' is an example of onomatopoeia.

2) For part b), think about the different types of imagery:

   I was like a rush-hour commuter on the Underground

   The key word is 'like' — the author compares their experience to being a rush-hour commuter. This is an example of a simile.

3) You need to find an example of an idiom in the passage for part c). Look for a phrase where the literal meaning is different to the intended meaning.

   ...I decided to call it a day after 45 minutes...

   The author didn't literally 'call it a day'. Instead, it means that they gave up and did something else. So 'call it a day' is an idiom.

Use the next few pages to test yourself on these techniques...

There are lots of techniques to get your head round in this section. Once you're confident that you know your metaphors from your alliteration, have a go at the practice questions over the page.

Section Four — Writers' Techniques

Practice Questions

It's time to get technical — answer these questions on the techniques from the previous section. There are a lot of oddly spelt words, but these questions should help you get the hang of them.

> Underline the words in each sentence that use the technique in brackets.
> Look at this example:
>
> **Example:** Ann's dress had several <u>fancy frills</u> and lace on the hems. **(alliteration)**

1. A loud crackle and a flash from the fire made Mr Cox jolt awake. **(onomatopoeia)**

2. Their chatter subsided until only the whistling wind could be heard. **(alliteration)**

3. The full moon shone through the cracks in the crumbling castle walls. **(alliteration)**

4. With a snap, the ruler broke and flew across the room. **(onomatopoeia)**

5. Joe was woken in the night by the croaking of the fat, green frogs. **(onomatopoeia)**

> Write a word or phrase to complete each sentence using the writers' technique in brackets. Look at this example:
>
> **Example:** Jay's smile was _as bright as the sun_ . **(simile)**

6. The fluffy clouds were _____ . **(simile)**

7. The cat's eyes were _____ . **(metaphor)**

8. Dasha walked _____ . **(simile)**

9. The evil man's heart was _____ . **(metaphor)**

10. Jamal climbed _____ . **(simile)**

Section Four — Writers' Techniques

Practice Questions

> Write down whether each sentence contains an analogy or personification. Look at this example:
>
> **Example:** The shredder devoured the paper greedily. __personification__

11. The old door let out a low groan as Cam pushed it open. _____

12. Finding my keys was like finding a needle in a haystack. _____

13. An icy wind bit the explorers' cheeks as they began their trek. _____

14. I'm not a very good dancer. There are statues less stiff than I am. _____

15. The fireworks were deafeningly loud — they boomed like bombs. _____

16. Dust danced and whirled through the air in the motorbike's wake. _____

> Write down whether the underlined part of each sentence is an abbreviation, an acronym or an initialism. Look at this example:
>
> **Example:** Kim was a training to be a vet. __abbreviation__

17. Tolu was sure there was a UFO in the sky. _____

18. We have a maths lesson every Thursday morning. _____

19. My brother and I went SCUBA diving in Barbados. _____

20. Marianne was treated like a VIP in the fancy hotel. _____

21. Josie couldn't wait to install the new app on her mobile phone. _____

Section Four — Writers' Techniques

Practice Questions

> Choose whether each sentence contains verbal irony (**VI**), situational irony (**SI**) or a rhetorical question (**RQ**). Underline your answer. Look at this example:
>
> **Example:** Would you like to hear about Britain's top microwave? (VI SI <u>RQ</u>)

22. For the first time ever, Fazia left home early, only for the bus to be late. (VI SI RQ)

23. Manu ended his speech by saying, "Are uniforms really needed?" (VI SI RQ)

24. After losing ten games, the manager was ecstatic with their performance. (VI SI RQ)

25. Mum said, "How many times do I have to tell you to set the table?" (VI SI RQ)

26. "Having a cold is a lot of fun," Dad said, blowing his nose. (VI SI RQ)

> Write down whether each phrase or sentence is an idiom or a cliché. Look at this example:
>
> **Example:** A bad workman always blames his tools. ____idiom____

27. And they all lived happily ever after. _____

28. My homework was a piece of cake. _____

29. I had the time of my life. _____

30. You're pulling my leg. _____

31. Go back to the drawing board. _____

32. Better late than never. _____

Section Four — Writers' Techniques

Practice Questions

> Write down a synonym for each underlined word. Look at this example:
> **Example:** Raj thought the party was nightmarish. ___horrible___

33. Jack's boss, Susan, had a very mysterious past. _____

34. The spiders spun webs in the darkness of the cellar. _____

35. Jennifer stared up at the impressive skyscraper. _____

36. All the systems on the aeroplane were operating normally. _____

37. The sculpture of the llama looked very realistic. _____

> Write down an antonym for each underlined word. Look at this example:
> **Example:** Laurie tidied the house frantically. ___calmly___

38. The attic is full of worthless things my family has collected. _____

39. There was a lack of carrots in the field that year. _____

40. The mysterious man's appearance was striking. _____

41. The gardens around the manor house were unkempt. _____

42. Miya's new plant was thriving on the windowsill. _____

Section Four — Writers' Techniques

Section Five — Comprehension

Reading the Text

Comprehension texts come in all shapes and sizes — here's how to tackle them...

Texts can be Divided into Fiction and Non-fiction

1) <u>Fiction</u> texts are <u>made up</u> by the author, and are about <u>imaginary events</u> and <u>people</u>. <u>Non-fiction</u> texts are based on <u>facts</u>, and are about <u>real people</u> and <u>events</u>.
2) Here are some <u>examples</u> of the types of texts you might get in your reading comprehension:

Fiction Texts

Novels or Short Stories	→	You could get a short story or an extract from a novel. These texts usually have a <u>plot</u>, <u>characters</u> and a <u>narrator</u>.
Myths or Legends	→	These are <u>traditional cultural stories</u> that often involve <u>supernatural beings</u> or <u>events</u>.
Poems	→	A poem is written in <u>lines</u>, not <u>prose</u>. Most poems have a <u>rhythm</u> and some may <u>rhyme</u>.
Film or Play Scripts	→	These are mostly made up of <u>dialogue</u>, with some <u>stage directions</u>. The speaking characters' names are listed on the left side.

Prose is the opposite of poetry — it's a continuous piece of writing.

Non-fiction Texts

Autobiographies or Biographies	→	These are <u>factual accounts</u> of a <u>real person's life</u>, either written by that person (autobiography) or by someone else (biography).
Reference Books	→	An <u>extract</u> from an <u>encyclopedia</u> or <u>history book</u> will give the reader an <u>explanation</u> or <u>information</u> about a <u>specific topic</u>.
Instructions	→	Instructions are often written as a <u>list</u>, e.g. a recipe.
Letters	→	Letters are <u>written correspondence</u> from <u>one person</u> to <u>another</u>.

Comprehension Questions ask you to Pick Out Details

EXAMPLE:

Method — Highlighting key words saves time

1) <u>Scan</u> the text for the <u>main points</u>, and <u>highlight</u> a few <u>key words</u>.
2) <u>Key words</u> are things that tell you <u>who</u>, <u>what</u>, <u>where</u>, <u>when</u>, <u>why</u> and <u>how</u>.

> Not much is known about the origins of Stonehenge. Nobody knows when it was erected, but most historians think that it must have happened between 3000 and 2000 BC. Equally, it is unclear why it was built; some scholars argue that it served a religious purpose, but others think that it was a kind of observatory, to study the movements of the stars and planets.

The purposes would be helpful in a 'why' question.

This tells you the subject of the passage.

The dates would be helpful in a 'when' question.

Reading the Text

Pay Attention to Key Words in the Question

EXAMPLE: Method — Use your highlighting to find the information you need

1) Read the questions about the passage — use question words like who, when and where to work out what information they are asking for.
2) Then, look back at the key words that you highlighted in the passage to find the information you need to answer the questions.

When does the text suggest Stonehenge was built?
— This question asks 'when', so you need to look for dates.
The passage says it was built 'between 3000 and 2000 BC'.

What reasons does the text give for its construction?
— This question asks 'what reasons', so you need to look for purposes.
The passage mentions a 'religious purpose' or use as an 'observatory'.

Practice Questions

1) Read the passage below and then answer the questions that follow.

> 1   Sonal couldn't believe her eyes. Standing in front of her was Oti Debuski, lead vocalist of 'The Volcanics'. Oti, otherwise known as Lavahead, wasn't wearing her trademark deerhunter and aviators, but there was no doubt about it. It was her all right! Sonal had worked here for two whole
> 5   years and this was the most exciting thing that had happened in all that time. She'd never met anyone famous before, and now she was meeting the frontwoman of her favourite band. It was astounding.
>   "Hey kid," Oti said commandingly, "you might want to try shutting that mouth." Sonal swallowed loudly. "S-S-Sorry," she stammered, as she
> 10 scanned through Oti's basket. Oti just stood back and gazed lazily, almost as if she were a normal person.

a) What is Oti Debuski's stage name?
b) What word in the passage can mean the same as 'lead vocalist' (line 2)?
c) What kind of place does Sonal work in?
d) Why do you think Oti tells Sonal to shut her mouth?
e) What evidence is there in the passage which suggests how Sonal was feeling?

TEST TIP — **Read the passage carefully before you write your answers...**
There's lots to read for the comprehension part of your test. Highlighting key information will help you find the bits you need quickly when you're ready to answer the questions.

Section Five — Comprehension

Understanding the Questions

Here are some lovely pages about 'Understanding the Questions' — just my cup of tea.

Make sure you Know the Different Question Types

1) You need to use different skills for different question types.
2) You should recognise question types so you know how to answer them.

The same question types come up in both standard answer and multiple choice tests. See p.86-87 for more about the two question styles.

Fact Recall Questions

Fact recall questions usually use words like who, where, what, when, why and how:

> What are the names of the two brothers?
> When did the ship set sail?

You should be able to find answers to questions like these simply by reading through the passage carefully.

EXAMPLE: Method — Find the facts

1) First, you need to look at the question to find out what you are looking for. You may need to read between the lines if the answer is not obvious.

   > Who is Georgina's oldest child?

   'Who' tells you that you're looking for a name. 'oldest' tells you to look for information about ages.

2) Scan the text for the information that will help you work out the answer.

   Wei is the youngest, so it can't be her. → Georgina had four children: Lily, Oscar, Toby and Wei. As the youngest, Wei was spoiled growing up, whilst Lily and Toby competed over who was the favourite middle child.

   The oldest must be one of these four.
   Lily and Toby are the middle children, so it can't be them.

3) This information shows that Oscar must be the oldest child.

Questions about Word Meanings

You might need to use your knowledge of word meanings to answer a question:

EXAMPLE: How did Nina feel about the state of the kitchen?

The key words in the question tell you what it is asking.

Method — Think about word meanings

1) Once you know what the question is asking, you can find the information in the text:

   > Nina was repulsed by what she saw in the kitchen. ← The text tells you how she feels.

2) If the question gives you options, choose the one that has the closest meaning:

   A She was delighted.
   B She was appalled.
   C She was disgusted.
   D She was confused.
   E She was astounded.

   Out of all the options 'disgusted' is the closest to 'repulsed', so C is the answer.

   See p.74-75 for more advice on questions about word meaning.

Section Five — Comprehension

Understanding the Questions

Multiple Statement Questions

You may be given a list of statements and asked which ones are right or wrong. You need to choose a letter from A to E that matches the right combination of options.

EXAMPLE: According to the text, which of these were Conservative prime ministers?

1. Margaret Thatcher   2. Tony Blair   3. Gordon Brown   4. John Major

A   1 and 2
B   2 and 3
C   2 and 4 ← You need to pick out the letter which matches the correct combination of options.
D   1 and 4
E   3 and 4

Some multiple statement questions just ask for one answer, e.g. 'Which of these statements is true?'

Method — Narrow down the options

You need to work out which two options are correct, using information from the text.

Here's one of the answers...

...and here's the other answer. So you need the letter which matches option 1 and 4 — letter D.

> The Conservative Party dominated British politics during the 1980s and early 1990s. Margaret Thatcher was Prime Minister from 1979 to 1990, followed by John Major from 1990 to 1997. After that, the Labour Party regained power with the election of Tony Blair. They remained in power led by Gordon Brown until 2010.

Reasoning Questions

Reasoning questions ask about the text's purpose or meaning.

1) These questions could use phrases like 'most likely' or ask you about the opinions of the author or characters.

You might need to use common sense to work out the answers to some reasoning questions.

EXAMPLE:

This question is asking about the text's purpose. →

> Why does Amira keep her prize a secret?
> What is the writer's view of wine in general?

← If a question asks about something that isn't in the text, look for clues in the information you're given.

2) Questions that ask 'why' or 'what do you think' might test your own opinion. Think about the impression you get from the text's language and tone.

Questions about Grammar and Literary Techniques

You might get a question about grammar and literary techniques:

See Section 1 and Section 4 for detailed advice on how to answer these types of question.

EXAMPLE: What type of word is 'tweeted'? ← Look at the sentence that the word is from to work out the answer.

Knowing the kinds of questions you'll face will help in the test...

There's no way of knowing what the questions in the test will be about, but you can learn what kinds of questions might appear. Make sure you've given these pages plenty of attention.

Section Five — Comprehension

Answering Comprehension Questions

Here are some cracking comprehension questions with advice on how to answer them.

Multiple Choice Questions give you Several Possible Options

1) In Multiple Choice questions the answer is always given. You just need to pick the right one.
2) When the possible options are similar, it can make the question more difficult. The best way to tackle each question is to work through it carefully, step by step.

EXAMPLE: Read the passage below. Then answer the question that follows.

> 1 The problem was not that the film was three hours long, or that the acting was atrocious, but that the plot was incomprehensible. I have no idea what Captain Jutter had to do with anything, partly because I could not understand a word she said, but also because she disappeared halfway
> 5 through the film, without any explanation. I don't think it was ever explained exactly why the pirates had to get back to Shadow Island; all I know is that it was of "great importance". The screenwriter, Jordan Vidal, needs to take a long, hard look in the mirror after this terrible mishap of an adventure film.

1) According to the passage, what was the film's main downfall?

    A The screenwriter was not very good.
    B The acting was terrible.
    C The story was too complicated.
    D It didn't make any sense.
    E It was too long.

Be wary of options that are mentioned in the text but don't answer the question, as they could mislead you. Always double-check that your answer matches the text.

Method — Find the important information

1) First, look for any key words relating to the question (you may have highlighted them during your first read-through):

    'problem' means the same as 'downfall'.

> The **problem** was not that the film was **three hours long**, or that the **acting was atrocious**, but that the **plot was incomprehensible**.

This sentence mentions three possible answers to the question.

The sentence tells you that the problem was not the length of the film or the acting, so it cannot be option B or E.

2) Check this information against the options.

    A The screenwriter was not very good.
    B ~~The acting was terrible.~~
    C The story was too complicated.
    D It didn't make any sense.
    E ~~It was too long.~~

Option C mentions the 'story', but says it was too complicated, which does not match the text.

Option D is closest in meaning to the text — 'incomprehensible' means 'doesn't make any sense'.

3) Double-check you haven't missed anything else. The last line of the passage does suggest that the screenwriter was not very good (option A), but D is still the best answer.

Section Five — Comprehension

Answering Comprehension Questions

Use Your Own Words for Standard Answer Questions

1) Standard Answer comprehension questions aren't too different from Multiple Choice questions.
2) You can find the answers in the same way, but instead of choosing a given answer, you need to put it into your own words and write in full sentences.
3) Read the extract on p.86, and then look at the question below.

EXAMPLE: 2) Explain why the writer found the plot "incomprehensible" (line 2).

Method — Ask yourself questions as you're reading

1) First, work out what information the question is asking you for:

   > Explain why the writer found the plot "incomprehensible" (line 2)?

   This gives you a clue to where to start looking for the answer.

   This tells you that you're looking for reasons why the writer didn't understand the story.

2) You should start by looking at the part of the text mentioned in the question:

   > I have no idea what Captain Jutter had to do with anything, partly because I could not understand a word she said, but also because she disappeared halfway through the film, without any explanation.

   This sentence comes straight after the writer mentions that the story was "incomprehensible".

   Finding key words will help you work out what's important.

   This sentence tells you that the writer did not know why Captain Jutter was in the film, because he could not understand what she said, and she disappeared halfway through.

3) After looking around line 2, you should then check the key words in the rest of the text:

   > I don't think it was ever explained exactly why the pirates had to get back to Shadow Island...

   The word 'explained' suggests that this sentence relates to the plot.

4) When you have the information, you need to rewrite it in full sentences, in your own words:

   > The plot was "incomprehensible" because the writer did not know why Captain Jutter was in the film, and found it impossible to understand her. The writer was also confused because Captain Jutter vanished in the middle of the film, and it was not explained why the pirates needed to go to Shadow Island.

   Quoting from the question helps focus your answer.

   Change the wording so you're not just copying the text.

5) Use the number of marks and space available for your answer as a guide for how much to write.

TEST TIP — Try to answer every question...

Don't spend too long on any one question — you don't want to run out of time. If you're not sure what the answer is, make a sensible guess and carry on to the next question.

Section Five — Comprehension

Practice Questions

Now it's time to put what you've learned into practice. There are two passages on these pages. One's non-fiction and the other is fiction — both have some questions for you to have a go at.

> Read the passage below, then answer the questions that follow.
> Underline the correct option for each question.
>
> **Example:** What does the word "transmitted" (line 1) mean?
>
>   **A** <u>passed</u>   **B** introduced   **C** meant   **D** turned

Eyam and the Great Plague

In 1665, Britain was hit by a dangerous disease called bubonic plague. It was transmitted to people by fleas (carried by rats). It could spread very quickly, so one village in Derbyshire took steps to try and protect nearby villages and towns.

Eyam was a rural village with just 800 residents. Plague had arrived in Eyam inside
5 a flea-infested box of cloth. Rather than deserting their home, residents decided to stay put and stop anyone coming into or going out of their village. This meant the plague couldn't spread any further. People from neighbouring villages would leave supplies just outside of Eyam for the villagers to collect, and money was left in special stones with vinegar-filled grooves, as vinegar was thought to kill infection on the coins' surfaces.

10 The village of Eyam is remembered to this day for its heroic and pragmatic response to the plague. The villagers helped to protect nearby towns, like Bakewell, by limiting the spread of the disease — it is thought that their courage saved thousands of lives.

1. How was the plague brought into Eyam?

   A on money   **B** by rats   **C** by fleas   **D** by a villager

2. According to the passage, villagers in Eyam tried to pay for deliveries safely by:

   A wrapping coins in cloth.   **C** disinfecting coins.
   B heating coins up.   **D** washing coins in water.

3. What does the word "pragmatic" (line 10) mean?

   A swift   **B** sensible   **C** tentative   **D** innovative

4. How do you think the author feels about the choice the villagers in Eyam made?

   A impressed   **B** delighted   **C** confused   **D** disappointed

Section Five — Comprehension

Practice Questions

Read the passage below, then answer the questions that follow.
Underline the correct option for each question.

Example: What did the twelve sisters travel in?

    A a boat   **B** a carriage   **C** <u>a basket</u>   **D** a cart

Abridged extract from 'The Celestial Sisters' by Cornelius Mathews

White Hawk lived in a remote part of the forest. Every day he returned from the chase with a large spoil, for he was one of the most skilful and lucky hunters of his tribe. His form was like the cedar; there was no forest too gloomy for him to penetrate, and no track made by bird or beast of any kind which he could not readily follow.

5   One day, after walking for some time, he suddenly came to a ring worn among the grass and the flowers, as if it had been made by footsteps moving lightly round and round. But it was strange — so strange as to cause White Hawk to pause and gaze long and fixedly upon the ground — there was no path which led to this flowery circle. There was not even a crushed leaf nor a broken twig, nor the least trace of a footstep.

10   Presently he heard the faint sounds of music in the air. He looked up in the direction they came from, and he saw a small object. As it neared the earth it appeared as a basket, and it was filled with twelve sisters, of the most lovely and enchanting beauty.

5. Which of the following statements is false?

   A White Hawk is a good explorer.   **C** White Hawk lives in an isolated area.
   B White Hawk's tribe has one hunter.   **D** White Hawk can track animals easily.

6. What does "a large spoil" (line 2) mean?

   A rotten food   **B** many weapons   **C** a large deer   **D** plenty of food

7. Which of these does White Hawk not expect to see as evidence that the ring was made by a person?

   A a path   **B** footsteps   **C** flowers   **D** damaged vegetation

8. Why does White Hawk look up in the last paragraph?

   A He wants to see the twelve sisters.   **C** He sees a small object in the sky.
   B He hears the sisters talking.   **D** He hears music.

Section Five — Comprehension

Section Six — Writing

How to Prepare for the Writing Test

Most people find creative writing tricky — follow the advice in this section and you'll be fine.

Work on your Vocabulary and Writing Style

Here are some ways you can improve your writing style before the test:

1) Read lots of books to develop your vocab and writing style. Read a range of things — fiction, non-fiction and poetry.
2) Write vocabulary lists of tricky words and their meanings — advanced vocabulary will help you to impress the examiners (as long as you use it correctly).
3) Make a list of useful techniques — e.g. comparison (see p.97) and personification (see p.67). Write down some examples of each to help you remember how to use them.
4) You could also jot down some useful phrases that you could use in almost any story. For example, general descriptions of surroundings — 'a quilted forest floor' or 'a picture of tranquillity'.

When you come across a word you don't know, look it up in a dictionary.

Prepare some Ideas Before the Test

1) Some topics come up often in the test. It will save you time if you've already thought about these — even if your question is different, you can adapt the stories you've prepared.

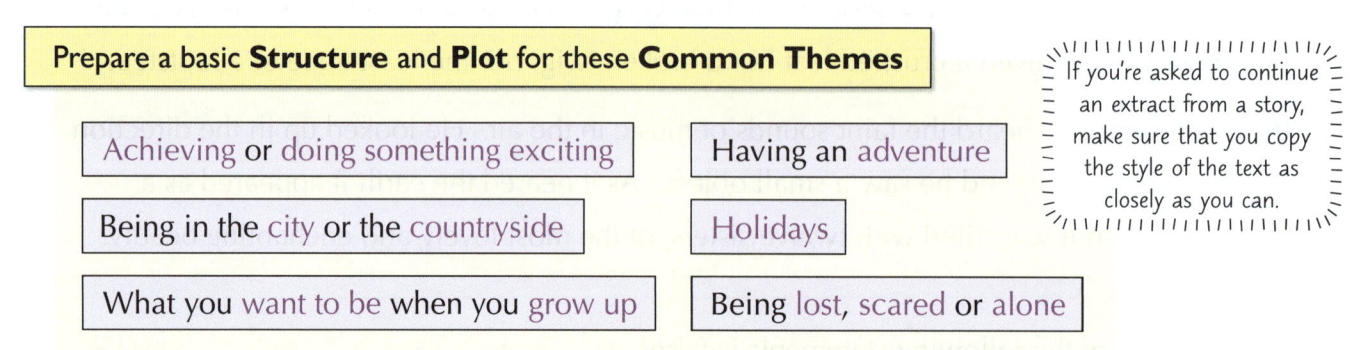

Prepare a basic Structure and Plot for these Common Themes

- Achieving or doing something exciting
- Being in the city or the countryside
- What you want to be when you grow up
- Having an adventure
- Holidays
- Being lost, scared or alone

If you're asked to continue an extract from a story, make sure that you copy the style of the text as closely as you can.

Think of Characters and Settings to include in your Writing

- Here are some ideas for characters you could use in lots of different stories:

  - A kind old lady
  - A strict teacher
  - A sporty teenager
  - A brave child

- Have a think about different settings too — your story could take place in:

  - A haunted house
  - A busy city
  - A desert island
  - An empty school

- Picture the character or place in your mind — think about what you can see and how you'd describe it. Think of some comparisons to make your descriptions interesting (see p.97), e.g. 'her fingers were like gnarled twigs' or 'The island was an emerald in a sapphire sea.'

2) Think of some ways to start and end a story too — you could start in the middle of the action to grab your reader's attention, and you could end with something unexpected (see p.92).

How to Prepare for the Writing Test

Read plenty of Non-fiction Texts

1) You might have to write a non-fiction text in the test — for example, a letter or newspaper article.
2) To help you prepare, read lots of non-fiction texts, for example adverts, articles in newspapers and magazines, and books about history or science.

Think about whether the Writer is trying to:

- Persuade you to do something (e.g. donate money, buy a product).

  > It is vital that these cats find a loving home. Haven't they suffered enough?

  ← Persuasive writing contains arguments. It might try to appeal to the reader's emotions.

- Inform you about a subject (e.g. a natural history book might tell you about dinosaurs).

  > Dinosaurs died out 65 million years ago, so scientists use fossils to learn about them.

  ← Informative writing contains facts. It might give numbers or statistics.

- Describe something (e.g. a travel journal might describe a foreign country).

  > The soft lights of Nice glittered like jewels across the dark sea.

  ← Descriptive writing is full of adjectives. It often goes into a lot of detail.

3) Use what you've read to help you with your own non-fiction writing. Think about what you're asked to write and whether you should persuade, inform or describe something to your reader.

Practise writing Letters

You might well be asked to write a letter in the test. Letters are just like any other type of writing, but you have to use the right style, and know how to start and end them properly.

Letters can be Formal or Informal

- Letters to people you don't know well, or somebody in charge, should use a formal style.

  These are both formal introductions: **Dear Sir/Madam** → **Yours faithfully** / **Dear Mrs Jones** → **Yours sincerely** These are both formal endings.

  Use 'Yours sincerely' if you use their name, 'Yours faithfully' if you don't.

- Letters to a friend or relative should use an informal style.

  This is an informal introduction: **Dear Birgit** → **Best wishes** or **See you soon** These are both informal endings.

Practise writing informal letters (e.g. to a relative or a penpal), and formal letters — for example to your local council to give your views on an issue such as the closure of a youth club.

Formal writing isn't too chatty and uses Standard English. Informal writing is more chatty (see page 20).

REVISION TIP — Practise different types of writing...

Don't just write stories — make sure you're comfortable writing non-fiction texts as well.

Section Six — Writing

Make a Plan

Like anything in life, it's important to have a good plan. 11+ English is no different...

Stories should have a Beginning, Middle and End

If you're writing a story, make sure you structure it clearly:

1) Beginning — your first paragraph has to grab the reader's attention.

   You could start by setting the scene... → It was a cold, dark November evening.

   ... or you could jump straight into the action. → The beast attacked again that night, leaving chaos in its wake.

   Writing a plan (see p.93) will help you work out the best structure for your story or essay.

2) Middle — build up your action. Make sure you've got at least one key event in your plan that you can describe in detail. Don't forget to write in paragraphs (see p.94).

   Suddenly I heard a pattering behind me. I spun around, and found myself looking into the glinting, red eyes of the beast.

   Make sure enough happens to keep your reader hooked, but don't forget to make your descriptions interesting.

3) End — make sure your story finishes with a paragraph that wraps up your plot.

   You could end with a twist to surprise your reader... → "There you are, Snowy," I said, scooping up my pet rabbit.

   ... or you could reflect on what your character has learnt. → From that day, Kemen was a changed boy. He became kind and thoughtful, and he never bullied anyone again.

Essays should have an Introduction, Argument and Conclusion

Structure is just as important if you're writing a non-fiction text, like an essay, letter or article:

1) Introduction — your first paragraph should explain what you're going to write about.

   Put forward your main argument... → Unhealthy food should not be sold in schools because it causes obesity.

   ... or if you're writing to inform, introduce your topic. → Durham is an ancient city in north-east England.

2) Argument — use the middle of the essay to back up your points and give detail.

   More than 25% of children in the UK are overweight, and 6% say that they are bullied because of their weight.

   If you're writing to persuade, use statistics to make your argument convincing.

3) Conclusion — use your last paragraph to summarise your points.

   Writing 'In conclusion' or 'In summary' makes it clear that this is the end of your essay. → In conclusion, if schools stopped selling unhealthy food then children would be healthier and happier, and would grow into healthy adults.

Section Six — Writing

Make a Plan

Write a **Plan** to **Structure** your **Answer**

Planning your essay will help you to structure your writing and write a better answer. The amount of time you spend planning will depend on the overall time limit for the writing task.

EXAMPLE: Write a story about an unusual event.

Read the question carefully — pick out what type of writing it's asking for, and what the topic is.

Method — Write a brief plan using bullet points

1) If you're short of time in the test, your plan should be very short.
2) Look at the question and spend a couple of minutes working out what to write about.
3) Write your plan in note form to save time.

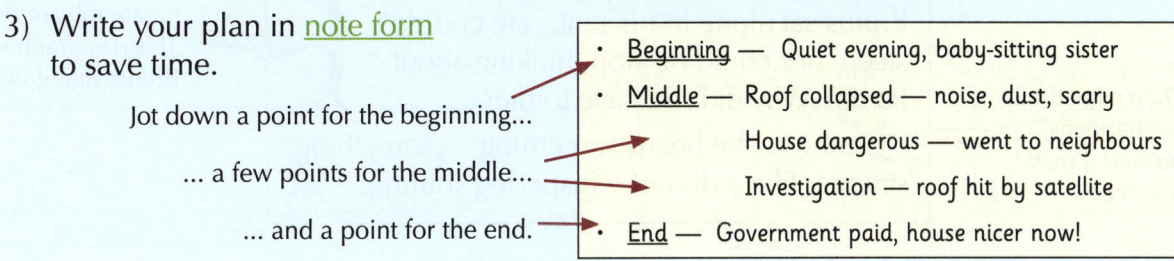

Jot down a point for the beginning...
... a few points for the middle...
... and a point for the end.

- Beginning — Quiet evening, baby-sitting sister
- Middle — Roof collapsed — noise, dust, scary
  - House dangerous — went to neighbours
  - Investigation — roof hit by satellite
- End — Government paid, house nicer now!

EXAMPLE: Write a story (real or made up) with the title 'Lost and Alone'.

Method — Use a spider diagram to plan your answer

1) If you've got more time, your essay will be longer, so your plan can be more detailed.
2) Decide what to write about, then jot down your ideas as notes or a spider diagram.
3) Spider diagrams are a good way to see how different ideas are connected.

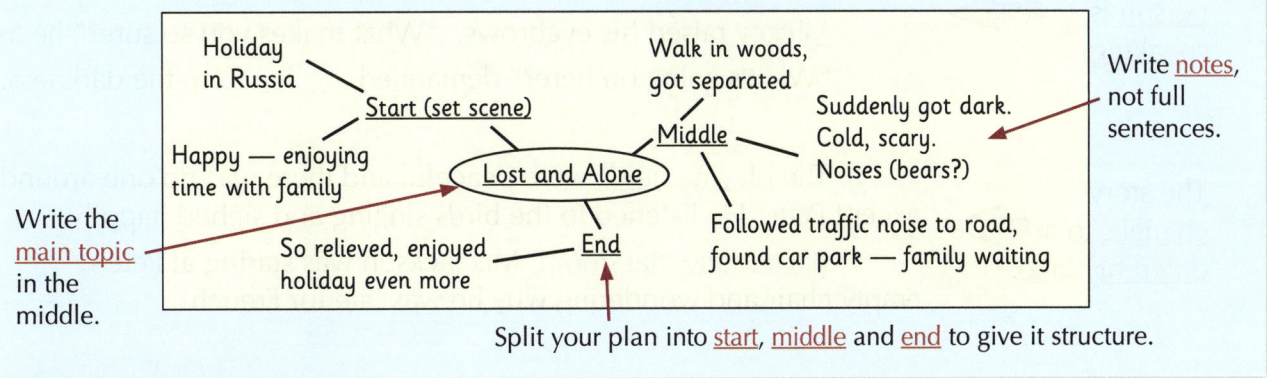

Write the main topic in the middle.

- Holiday in Russia
- Happy — enjoying time with family
- Start (set scene)
- **Lost and Alone**
- Walk in woods, got separated
- Middle
- Suddenly got dark. Cold, scary. Noises (bears?)
- Followed traffic noise to road, found car park — family waiting
- End
- So relieved, enjoyed holiday even more

Write notes, not full sentences.

Split your plan into start, middle and end to give it structure.

Practice Questions

1) Write down a plan of five bullet points for each of the questions below.
   a) Write an article arguing that driving lessons should be given at secondary school.
   b) Write a story with 'A Surprise Party' as the title.

TEST TIP: Keep checking your plan as you write...
This will help you to keep your writing focused and stop you from getting sidetracked.

Section Six — Writing

Write in Paragraphs

Paragraphs are pretty important — without them, your writing would just be one big splurge of words. Make sure you use them correctly in the test by following these simple rules.

Use Paragraphs to Introduce Something New

1) A paragraph is a group of sentences that talk about the same thing, or follow on from each other.
2) All of the sentences in a paragraph should be related to each other.
3) Start a new paragraph every time something changes.

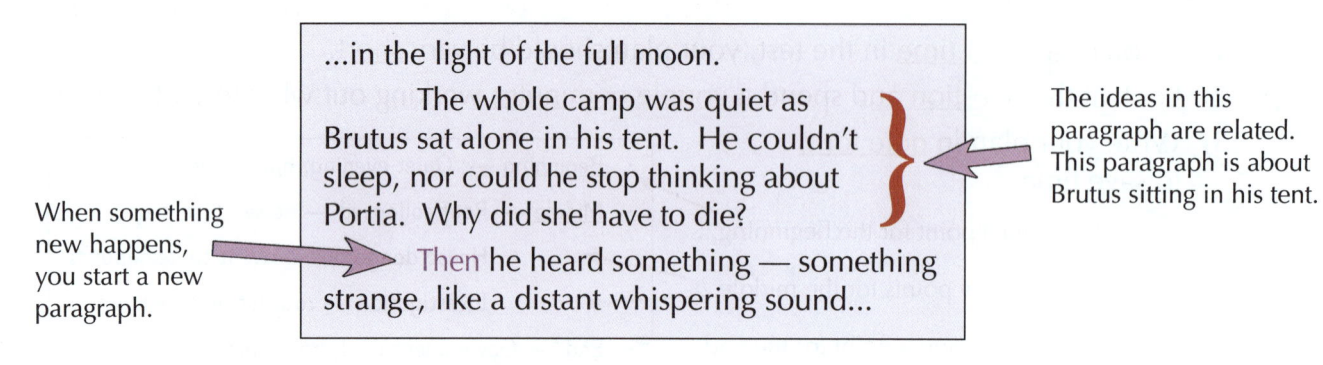

> ...in the light of the full moon.
>
> The whole camp was quiet as Brutus sat alone in his tent. He couldn't sleep, nor could he stop thinking about Portia. Why did she have to die?
>
> Then he heard something — something strange, like a distant whispering sound...

When something new happens, you start a new paragraph.

The ideas in this paragraph are related. This paragraph is about Brutus sitting in his tent.

Know When to Use a New Paragraph

Start a New Paragraph When...

A different person is speaking.

> "I'll find him," muttered Donald. "He won't get away this time, wherever he hides."
>
> Mickey raised his eyebrows. "What makes you so sure?" he asked.
>
> "What's going on here?" demanded a voice from the darkness.

The story changes to a different place.

> The playing fields were peaceful and there was no one around except Pete. He listened to the birds singing and sighed happily.
>
> Back in the classroom, Mrs Jackson was staring at Pete's empty chair and wondering why he was late for French.

The story changes to a different time.

> By five o'clock, Evka was angry. Shirley was late again, and the flower she'd bought was starting to droop.
>
> Six o'clock came, and she still hadn't appeared. Enough was enough. Stuffing her flower into a bin, Evka went home.

The action of the story changes.

> Lauren kicked her feet through the dead leaves and reached down to pick up a stick to throw for Barney. It was then that she heard it.
>
> The growl of a motorbike engine could clearly be heard approaching along the path through the woods.

Section Six — Writing

Write in Paragraphs

Make sure that you Show New Paragraphs Clearly

EXAMPLE: Rewrite the text below, putting in new paragraphs where they belong.

> Emily stood at the side of the court, watching her team slump to another defeat. As soon as the half-time buzzer went, she stormed into the dressing room. The players watched her leave. "She doesn't look too happy," commented Harriet, the team's top scorer. As the team entered the dressing room, Emily was pacing up and down, muttering to herself. "Pathetic. Pathetic!" she shouted at the team as they sat down. Fifteen minutes later, the team came back on the court. Perhaps this time Emily's half-time talk would make a difference.

Method — Look for things that change

1) Read the passage <u>one sentence</u> at a time, working out where new paragraphs belong.

The first sentence should begin a paragraph.

Harriet is a new speaker.

> // Emily stood at the side of the court, watching her team slump to another defeat. As soon as the half-time buzzer went, she stormed into the dressing room. The players watched her leave. // "She doesn't look too happy," commented Harriet, the team's top scorer. // As the team entered the dressing room, Emily was pacing up and down, muttering to herself. "Pathetic. Pathetic!" she shouted at the team as they sat down. // Fifteen minutes later, the team came back on the court. Perhaps this time Emily's half-time talk would make a difference.

The dressing room is a new place.

This is a new time.

2) Once you work out where the <u>new paragraphs should start</u>, <u>rewrite</u> the passage. Show new paragraphs by <u>starting</u> a <u>new line</u> and <u>leaving a gap before</u> the <u>first sentence</u>.

Add a space at the beginning of the paragraph.

> ...watched her leave.
>   "She doesn't look too happy," commented Harriet, the team's top scorer.

Start a new line.

Practice Questions

1) Divide this text into paragraphs. Write // where a new paragraph should start.

> Following another run-in with Mr Ulrich, Gary had awaited his verdict nervously. "Gary, this is the third time you've been sent to my office for lateness. You should know better," the headmaster said, "but I know the perfect punishment — Miss Levis needs help with the junior hockey team." That was a month ago, and since then Gary had been coming to the threadbare pitch every week to help with coaching. It was a task he didn't enjoy — he disliked the children and he despised standing in the cold watching them play. There was one child he truly hated: Brenda. She had been a nuisance from the start. She tied Gary's shoelaces together when he wasn't looking and took every opportunity to hit the ball at him. "Stupid kids!" thought Gary, as it started to rain. "Stupid, rotten, silly kids!"

Revise the four main reasons you should start a new paragraph...

Go over these pages until you can work out where new paragraphs should start in your sleep.

Section Six — Writing

Make It Interesting

Your reader likes an interesting story as much as the next person — so make it interesting.

Don't Use the Same Words over and over again

Use different words with similar meanings to make your writing interesting (see p.74-75).

Different Adjectives

1) Adjectives are a good way to make your writing interesting, but using the same adjectives, like 'weird' or 'nice', gets repetitive:

   > I went to a nice Indian restaurant last night. I had an onion bhaji to start with and it was really nice. Then I had a nice curry.

   See p.10 for more on adjectives.

   This is written correctly, but repeating the word 'nice' makes it boring.

2) Using different adjectives makes all the difference:

   > I went to a great Indian restaurant last night. I had an onion bhaji to start with and it was really tasty. Then I had a delicious curry.

   This is the same piece of writing, but it's much more interesting.

Different Verbs

Using different verbs that mean similar things will make your writing more interesting than if you use the same ones over and over again.

See p.7 for more on verbs.

> I ran to the postbox with a letter, then I ran home so I wasn't late for tea.

→

> I hurried to the postbox with a letter, then I raced home so I wasn't late for tea.

These sentences are better because the verbs are more interesting. The verbs have slightly different meanings, but the stories stay the same.

> She jumped through the open window, and then jumped over the sleeping dog.

→

> She leaped through the open window, and then bounded over the sleeping dog.

Different Linking Words

1) Don't use the same words to link several parts of a sentence. E.g. You can avoid using conjunctions like 'and' by using different punctuation, such as commas and full stops:

   See p.18 for more on conjunctions.

   > I went to the beach and I put on my trunks and I walked to the sea and the water was warm and I swam for an hour.

   →

   > I went to the beach, put on my trunks and walked to the sea. The water was warm and I swam for an hour.

2) You could also use different linking words or change the order of the words:

   > We went to the bank then we had a coffee, then we went back to the car. Then we drove to the supermarket to do some shopping.

   →

   > After going to the bank, we had a coffee. Then we went back to the car and drove to the supermarket to do some shopping.

Section Six — Writing

Make It Interesting

Comparisons can create Clear Imagery

1) Comparisons help the reader to picture something more clearly.

| It was very cold. | ➡ | It was colder than an Arctic winter. | ⬅ This helps you imagine how cold it was. |

2) You can exaggerate (make something out to be more than it really is) to stress a point:

| Jack is as tall as a tree. | ⬅ Jack isn't really as tall as most trees, but your reader will understand, as long as your comparisons don't go over the top. |

There are Two Main Ways of Comparing

Don't use 'more' and '-er' or 'most' and '-est' together, e.g. 'most tallest' — stick to one or the other.

Less Than, More Than

You can make a comparison by saying 'more ... than', 'less ... than', 'most' or 'least', or you can use the form of the word that ends in '-er' or '-est'.

Ted is more sporty than Helen. ➡ Ted is sportier than Helen.

He is the most sporty person I know. ➡ He is the sportiest person I know.

Say that One Thing is Like Another

These are similes (see p.66) — using them will make your writing more interesting.

Another way of comparing is to say one thing is like another.
1) You can do this by using the word 'like'.

Her eyes lit up like the sky on bonfire night.   Soon my fingers were like blocks of ice.

2) You can also use 'as ... as':

He was as happy as a lark.   The idea was as useless as a chocolate teapot.

Revise these Useful Comparative Words

Words like 'best', 'worst' and 'most' are called superlatives.

Use these words to show how things are related to one another:

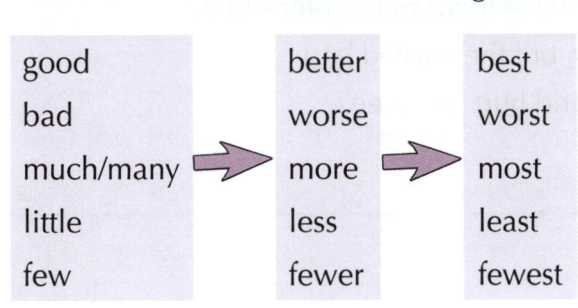

good	better	best
bad	worse	worst
much/many	more	most
little	less	least
few	fewer	fewest

Balal is good at writing stories, but Rosa is better.

Kell knows more card games than me, but Ali knows the most.

Maria made few mistakes in the test, Leah made fewer than Maria, and I made the fewest.

Section Six — Writing

Make It Interesting

Use **Different Types** of **Sentences**

1) Starting every sentence the same way can sound dull. Begin each sentence in a different way:

| There was nobody around as Palesa knocked on the door. There was a scream from inside. | → | Nobody was around as Palesa knocked on the door. A scream came from inside. |

← This is much better.

2) Use a variety of long and short sentences. Short sentences make descriptions sound exciting whereas long sentences make descriptions sound thoughtful:

I was walking to the station. I had to catch a train. It left at one. I was late. I began to run.
← These are too short.

I was walking to the station because I had to catch a train which left at one, and I was late, so I began to run.
← This is too long.

I was walking to the station because I had to catch a train which left at one. I was late, so I began to run.
← This is a good mix of long and short.

Add or **Replace Words** to make your **Sentences Better**

EXAMPLE:

Without changing the meaning of each sentence, add or replace at least two words to make the sentences more interesting.

a) We stayed inside because of the weather.
b) "That sounds like a deal!" said Mr Tibbs.

Method — Think of synonyms or adjectives

a) We stayed inside because of the terrible icy weather.
← You could add some adjectives to this sentence.

b) "That sounds like a great deal!" exclaimed old Mr Tibbs.
← You could replace the verb 'said' and add some adjectives to make this more interesting.

Practice Questions

1) Rewrite these sentences, adding at least two adjectives to make them more interesting.
   a) They went out to the park and played on the swings, the slide and the roundabout.
   b) Mr Brown told his cats to stay inside, but they never listened to him.

2) Replace the underlined words in these sentences to make them more interesting.
   a) We ate all the sausages because we were hungry, but they tasted bad.
   b) I ran to the cinema, but it was so dark that I fell and hurt my knee.

REVISION TIP — Get in a bit of extra practice...
Think of a synonym for each underlined word in Q2, then write a sentence that uses it.

Section Six — Writing

Writing Practice

The best way to polish your writing skills is to practise — here are some questions to start you off.

Writing Techniques

1) Rewrite these extracts to make them more interesting. Add or replace words, join together sentences that are too short and break up sentences that are too long.
    a) It was a nice day. I walked to the beach. I made a sandcastle. I ate an ice cream.
    b) The ogre was ugly and I felt scared and so I hid behind a rock until he left.
    c) "Quick, give me the fishing rod!" I said. I had seen a movement under the water. "Here you go," said Timmy, throwing me the rod. "It might not be strong enough. The Loch Ness monster is big. Here, take the net as well."

2) Write a comparison to say that each of these things is like something else.
    a) The sky was like...   b) The meal was as hot as...   c) His hair was like...

Writing Fiction

1) Write five words to describe each of these characters:
    a) an evil wizard.   b) a helpful lollipop man.   c) a talking bear.

2) Now write a description of the place where each character in question (1) lives.

3) Write a plan for each of the following questions:
    a) Write a short story with 'Extreme Weather' as the title.
    b) Read the extract on p.95 about Emily's half-time team talk. Continue the story from the end of the passage, explaining what happened next.

4) Choose one of the questions from (3). Use your plan to help you write the full story.

Writing Non-fiction

1) Write a plan for each of the following questions:
    a) Write a letter to a friend informing them about the pros and cons of owning a pet.
    b) Write a letter to your headteacher arguing against pupils having to wear uniforms.
    c) Write a journal entry describing what you did on your holidays.

2) Choose one of the questions from (1). Use your plan to help you write the full essay.

TEST TIP — **Check your writing for any errors...**
If you have time at the end of a writing task, read through what you've written and correct any mistakes. In particular, look out for spelling, punctuation and grammar errors.

Section Six — Writing

Practice Questions

Here are two pages of questions to really test your writing skills. If you're struggling for ideas, look back over the section — and remember to always use suitable vocabulary for the task.

> Complete each sentence in an exciting or interesting way. Look at this example:
>
> **Example:** Sonia walked up the steps, *flinching nervously as they creaked.*

1. Faisa followed the dog _____

2. I leapt over the gate _____

3. The horse neighed _____

4. Everyone cheered _____

5. Drake drank his tea _____

6. Elle opened the box _____

> Pick one of the titles or opening sentences below and write a brief plan for the story on a separate piece of paper. Use your plan to write a story. Write about 500 words.

7. Write a story with the title 'Moving House'.

8. Write a story with the title 'The Big Competition'.

9. Write a story with the title 'Shipwrecked on a Desert Island'.

10. Write a story with the title 'The Magic Necklace'.

11. Write a story that starts with the sentence "I tiptoed downstairs to investigate the source of the icy wind whistling through the house — the back door was wide open!"

Section Six — Writing

Practice Questions

> Write a sentence arguing **for** and **against** each statement. Look at this example:
>
> **Example:** Schools should teach children how to cook.
>
> **For:** Cooking is a useful life skill.
>
> **Against:** Ingredients can be expensive.

12. People should not be allowed to talk in libraries.

    For: _____

    Against: _____

13. Children should have to help out with housework around the home.

    For: _____

    Against: _____

14. Schools should offer all students a trip overseas.

    For: _____

    Against: _____

> Pick one of the essay prompts below and write a brief plan for the essay. Use your plan to write a full answer. Write about 500 words.

15. Write a newspaper article informing people about the plans the school council has been making to improve the school.

16. Write a letter to your headteacher persuading them to hold an end-of-term party.

17. Children should play a sport every day. Do you agree? Write an essay explaining the reasons for your answer.

18. Write an essay describing your favourite place to visit.

Section Six — Writing

Mixed Practice Tests

If you want to attempt each mixed practice test more than once, you will need to print **multiple-choice answer sheets** for these questions from our website — go to www.cgpbooks.co.uk/11plusanswersheets. Otherwise, circle the **correct answer** from the options **A** to **E**.

Give yourself **20 minutes** to complete this test. Write down your score in the box at the end.

Test 1

Read this poem carefully and answer the questions that follow.

The Blue Mountains

Above the ashes straight and tall,
Through ferns with moisture dripping,
I climb beneath the sandstone wall,
My feet on mosses slipping.

5 Like ramparts round the valley's edge
The tinted cliffs are standing,
With many a broken wall and ledge,
And many a rocky landing.

And round about their rugged feet
10 Deep ferny dells* are hidden
In shadowed depths, whence dust and heat
Are banished and forbidden.

The stream that, crooning to itself,
Comes down a tireless rover,
15 Flows calmly to the rocky shelf,
And there leaps bravely over.

Now pouring down, now lost in spray
When mountain breezes sally,
The water strikes the rock midway,
20 And leaps into the valley.

Now in the west the colours change,
The blue with crimson blending;
Behind the far Dividing Range***,
The sun is fast descending.

25 And mellowed day comes o'er the place,
And softens ragged edges;
The rising moon's great placid face
Looks gravely o'er the ledges.

by Henry Lawson

*dells — *small valleys*
**sally — *advance / charge*
***Dividing Range — *a mountain range in Australia*

Answer these questions about the text that you've just read. Circle the letter of the correct answer.

1. Which adjective best describes the ferns in verse 1?

    A   Upright
    B   Tall
    C   Damp
    D   Delicate
    E   Orderly

Mixed Practice Tests

Mixed Practice Tests

2. What are the "tinted cliffs" (line 6) compared to?

   A   Soldiers
   B   The defensive walls of a castle
   C   Large buildings
   D   Walls made from sandstone
   E   Tall trees

3. What type of word is "rugged" (line 9)?

   A   Proper noun
   B   Adverb
   C   Common noun
   D   Adjective
   E   Verb

4. Which of these statements is false?

   A   It is cooler in the valleys.
   B   The valleys have plenty of shade.
   C   There is a lot of dust in the valleys.
   D   The cliffs above the valleys are rocky.
   E   There are ferns in the valleys.

5. "The stream that, crooning to itself" (line 13). What is this phrase an example of?

   A   Onomatopoeia
   B   Personification
   C   A cliché
   D   Alliteration
   E   A simile

6. Which of the following is not mentioned in verse 5?

   A   It begins to rain heavily.
   B   The stream is now a waterfall.
   C   There is a wind blowing.
   D   The water bounces off a rock.
   E   The water continues to flow into the valley.

7. What do lines 25-26 say about how the landscape changes?

   A   It's much harsher in the evening light.
   B   The rock feels softer at night.
   C   The evening light makes the rocky landscape look gentler.
   D   The cliffs are not as beautiful in the evening.
   E   The valley looks scary at night.

8. Which of these is closest in meaning to the word "placid" (line 27)?

   A   Pale
   B   Calm
   C   Serious
   D   Graceful
   E   Impressive

Mixed Practice Tests

In this passage, there are some spelling mistakes. Circle the letter which matches the part of the sentence with the mistake. If there's no mistake, circle N.

9. Renowned for its / vibrent stripes of colour, / Peru's Rainbow Mountain / is a popular tourist
   A — B — C — D — N

10. attraction. / The lovely aray of colours / is caused by the minerals / which are abundant on
    A — B — C — D — N

11. its ridges and slopes. / This phenomenon / only became visible / in recent years after the
    A — B — C — D — N

12. snow melted away, / revealing the spectaculer / landscape beneath. / If you want to see this
    A — B — C — D — N

13. natural wander / though, you have to brave / the high altitude / and unpredictable weather.
    A — B — C — D — N

Choose the right words or phrases to complete this passage. Circle the letter which matches the correct word.

14. Rebecca glanced **at / on / up / over / in** her watch. She had an hour to explore the island
    A   B   C   D   E

15. before the boat left. She took off her sandals and **run / running / runned / ran / runs** across
    A   B   C   D   E

16. the beach, wincing slightly **because / caused / as for / for / due to** the hot sand. Not far
    A   B   C   D   E

17. from the beach, she found a lagoon **hidden / hid / hide / hided / hides** amongst the trees.
    A   B   C   D   E

18. She dipped her toes in first, **after / then / before / during / until** sinking into the cool water.
    A   B   C   D   E

Total (out of 18):

Mixed Practice Tests

Give yourself **20 minutes** to complete this test. Write down your score in the box at the end.

Test 2

Read this passage carefully and answer the questions that follow.

An extract from 'Sense and Sensibility'

The whole country about them abounded in beautiful walks and towards one of the hills did Marianne and Margaret one memorable morning direct their steps. They ascended the hills, and when they caught in their faces the animating gales of a high south-westerly wind, they pitied the fears which had prevented their mother and Elinor from sharing such delightful sensations. They
5   pursued their way against the wind, resisting it with laughing delight, when suddenly the clouds united over their heads, and a driving rain set full in their face. Chagrined* and surprised, they were obliged to turn back, for no shelter was nearer than their own house. One consolation however remained for them; it was that of running with all possible speed down the steep side of the hill which led immediately to their garden gate.
10   They set off. Marianne had at first the advantage, but a false step brought her suddenly to the ground; and Margaret, unable to stop herself to assist her, was involuntarily hurried along, and reached the bottom in safety. A gentleman was passing up the hill and within a few yards of Marianne, when her accident happened. He ran to her assistance. She had raised herself from the ground, but her foot had been twisted in her fall, and she was scarcely able to stand. The gentleman
15 took her up in his arms and carried her down the hill. Then passing through the garden, he bore her directly into the house and quitted not his hold till he had seated her in a chair in the parlour.
    Elinor and her mother rose up in amazement at their entrance, and the eyes of both were fixed on him with an evident wonder and a secret admiration which equally sprung from his appearance.

*Chagrined — *irritated*   **by Jane Austen**

Answer these questions about the text that you've just read.
Circle the letter of the correct answer.

1. The phrase "abounded in" (line 1) could most accurately be replaced by:
    A   was cursed with.
    B   had plenty of.
    C   was overwhelmed by.
    D   was bordered with.
    E   was surprised by.

2. Why didn't their mother and Elinor join Marianne and Margaret on the walk?
    A   They don't enjoy walking.
    B   They were afraid.
    C   They were too tired.
    D   They were scared of getting lost.
    E   They couldn't leave the parlour.

Mixed Practice Tests

3. Which of these is closest in meaning to the word "driving" (line 6)?

    A   Howling
    B   Sudden
    C   Frightening
    D   Forceful
    E   Changeable

4. Why do Marianne and Margaret decide to turn around and go home?

    A   The wind picks up speed.
    B   Margaret is tired of walking.
    C   They want to get out of the rain.
    D   They wanted to go back to see Elinor and their mother.
    E   They wanted to run down the steep hill.

5. What type of word is "yards" (line 12)?

    A   Verb
    B   Adjective
    C   Adverb
    D   Proper noun
    E   Common noun

6. Which of the following statements is false?

    A   Going down the hill, Marianne was initially ahead of Margaret.
    B   The gentleman was walking up the hill the girls were running down.
    C   Marianne hurt her foot.
    D   Marianne was unable to get up.
    E   The gentleman carried Marianne home.

7. Why was Margaret unable to help Marianne?

    A   She wasn't strong enough to carry Marianne.
    B   She had hurt her foot as well.
    C   She couldn't stop herself.
    D   She couldn't see Marianne through the rain.
    E   She was distracted by the gentleman.

8. "the eyes of both were fixed on him with an evident wonder and a secret admiration which equally sprung from his appearance" (lines 17-19).
   What do these lines mean?

    A   Elinor and her mother knew who the gentleman was.
    B   The gentleman's appearance horrified Elinor and her mother.
    C   Elinor and her mother were grateful to the gentleman.
    D   Elinor and her mother found the gentleman attractive.
    E   The gentleman was admiring Elinor and her mother.

Mixed Practice Tests

> In this passage, there are some spelling mistakes. Circle the letter which matches the part of the sentence with the mistake. If there's no mistake, circle N.

9. Ducks usually lay their eggs from March onwards. It takes approximately a month for the
      A   B   C   D   N

10. ducklings to hatch. During this critical stage, the female duck stays dutifly on her nest,
       A   B   C   D   N

11. only abandoning her post to forege for food. Once they are a little older, ducklings can
       A   B   C   D   N

12. feed themselves. However, they are particularly vulnerable to predaters, so stay close to
       A   B   C   D   N

13. their mother. After two months, they are fully fledged and ready for independense.
       A   B   C   D   N

> This passage contains some mistakes involving capital letters and punctuation. Circle the letter which matches the part of the sentence with the mistake. If there's no mistake, circle N.

14. The day of Romesh's flight to Moscow had finally arrived. He had borrowed his friends
       A   B   C   D   N

15. phrase book and had learnt some useful Russian words. In preparation for the cold he had
       A   B   C   D   N

16. packed; four woolly jumpers, a pair of gloves and some cosy earmuffs. He now felt a bit
       A   B   C   D   N

17. silly dressed in his winter-clothes at the airport — it was swelteringly hot. When his flight
       A   B   C   D   N

18. was announced, he felt a surge of excitement. He couldn't wait for the adventure to begin!
       A   B   C   D   N

Total (out of 18):

Mixed Practice Tests

Give yourself **20 minutes** to complete this test. Write down your score in the box at the end.

Test 3

Read this passage carefully and answer the questions that follow.

Venice

Venice, a city in north-east Italy, is a magical place. It's made up of 118 natural and man-made islands linked by hundreds of bridges. Wooden stilts were used as the foundations for buildings, leading to Venice being called a 'floating city'. Tourists flock to survey its winding canals, admire the historic houses with doors opening directly onto the water, and eat and drink in its many paved
5 squares. Several of its attractions are world-renowned, including the Grand Canal, the Bridge of Sighs — where prisoners crossed to their prison cells after being interrogated — and St. Mark's Basilica, an ornate cathedral.

Architecture isn't all that Venice is known for though. The city has a long tradition as an international centre of culture and business, and many of its customs continue today. A carnival is
10 held every year, where participants wear elaborate masks adorned with feathers, bells and sequins. Historically, Venetians were amongst the finest glass-blowers in the world, and many tourists still take home examples of this exquisite coloured glass as souvenirs. Visitors may also take a trip in a sleek black gondola (a long, canoe-like boat), punted along by a singing guide known as a gondolier.

Unfortunately, Venice faces a number of threats to its future. The increased pollution from large
15 cruise ships is a real challenge, but perhaps most worryingly, Venice is believed to be very slowly sinking. Over time, the soft seabed beneath the city has been compacting, meaning each year Venice drops 1-2 mm further into the sea. This problem has been intensified by rising sea levels. Every year floodwaters submerge many of the streets, and some predict the city could be uninhabitable by 2100. Venice's leaders have tried to stop the issue by building barriers to prevent tidal surges entering the
20 city, but the much-loved destination is still at risk of becoming nothing but a fairytale.

Answer these questions about the text that you've just read.
Circle the letter of the correct answer.

1. According to the passage, why is Venice known as a 'floating city'?

   A   It is drifting away from the rest of Italy.
   B   The main mode of transport is by boat.
   C   Its buildings are built upon wooden stilts.
   D   Many of the buildings are on floating platforms.
   E   You can only reach it by crossing the sea.

2. Which of these words best describes how Venice is presented in lines 3-5?

   A   Bustling
   B   Peaceful
   C   Dirty
   D   Sprawling
   E   Infamous

Mixed Practice Tests

3. The passage says "Several of its attractions are world-renowned" (line 5). What does this mean?

    A   Venice has more tourist attractions than any other country.
    B   Lots of places in Venice have won prizes.
    C   Venice receives tourists from all over the world.
    D   Not many people know about the best places in Venice.
    E   Many places in Venice are well-known in the rest of the world.

4. What type of word is "international" (line 9)?

    A   Adjective
    B   Proper noun
    C   Verb
    D   Adverb
    E   Abstract noun

5. Which of these is not mentioned as an activity you can do in Venice?

    A   Eating and drinking in one of the city's squares
    B   Learning how to punt a gondola
    C   Buying some of the coloured glass
    D   Seeing the historical houses by the water
    E   Admiring the canals

6. What does the word "elaborate" (line 10) mean?

    A   Luxurious
    B   Enchanting
    C   Detailed
    D   Expensive
    E   Antique

7. Which of these is closest in meaning to the word "intensified" (line 17)?

    A   Alleviated
    B   Improved
    C   Altered
    D   Heightened
    E   Eliminated

8. According to the passage, why might Venice become uninhabitable by 2100?

    A   Many of the bridges have started to collapse.
    B   The city is prone to flooding, which could get worse.
    C   There aren't enough barriers to stop tidal surges.
    D   Too many tourists are visiting Venice.
    E   The foundations of the city are crumbling.

Mixed Practice Tests

> This passage contains some mistakes involving capital letters and punctuation. Circle the letter which matches the part of the sentence with the mistake. If there's no mistake, circle N.

9. "I'll have three scoops please; one vanilla, one mint and one chocolate," Mark said with
       A   B   C   D   N

10. glee. Smiling broadly, the shopkeeper (Mr potter) handed Mark his ice-cream cone.
        A   B   C   D   N

11. "Watch out for Beaker the swan", he warned. "He loves stealing people's ice cream!"
        A   B   C   D   N

12. Mark chuckled to himself: he'd never heard of a swan that ate ice cream. Suddenly, he felt
        A   B   C   D   N

13. a sharp peck at his fingers. His ice cream was gone and in it's place was a satisfied swan.
        A   B   C   D   N

> Choose the right words or phrases to complete this passage. Circle the letter which matches the correct word.

14. Syrian hamsters make excellent pets if cared **for after with over by** properly.
                                                                A   B   C   D   E

15. **Although In spite While Even though Despite** their small size, they need a large home.
        A   B   C   D   E

16. When you bring your new furry friend home, **let letting allow allowed permitting**
                                                                                A   B   C   D   E

17. them to acclimatise to their new cage **before prior after next during** to playing with
                                                           A   B   C   D   E

18. them. Once they feel comfortable, you **can cannot have are ought** build them mazes
                                                                   A   B   C   D   E

    to encourage them to explore.

Total (out of 18):

Mixed Practice Tests

Give yourself **20 minutes** to complete this test. Write down your score in the box at the end.

Test 4

Read this passage carefully and answer the questions that follow.

An adapted extract from 'From the Earth to the Moon'

The first of December had arrived! The fateful day! For, if the projectile* were not launched that very night at 40 seconds past 10:48 pm, more than eighteen years must roll by before the moon would again present herself under the same conditions of her angle and proximity to Earth.

Ten o'clock struck! The moment had arrived for Barbicane and the others to take their
5 places in the projectile. Barbicane had regulated his chronometer** to the tenth part of a second by that of Murchison the engineer, who was charged with the duty of firing the gun by means of an electric spark. Thus, the travellers enclosed within the projectile were enabled to follow with their eyes the impassive needle which marked the precise moment of their departure.

The moment had arrived for saying "goodbye!" The scene was a touching one. Even
10 J. T. Maston had found in his own dry eyes one ancient tear, which he had doubtless reserved for the occasion.

A terrible silence weighed upon the entire scene. Not a breath of wind blew upon the earth. Not a sound of breathing came from the countless chests of the spectators. Their hearts seemed afraid to beat. All eyes were fixed upon the yawning mouth of the Columbiad***.
15 Murchison followed with his eye the hand of his chronometer. It wanted scarce forty seconds to the moment of departure, but each second seemed to last an age.

"Thirty-five. Thirty-six. Thirty-seven. Thirty-eight. Thirty-nine. Forty. FIRE!"

Instantly Murchison pressed with his finger the key of the electric battery and discharged the spark into the breech of the Columbiad.

by Jules Verne

*projectile — *a missile that can be launched, like a rocket*
**chronometer — *a precise clock*
***Columbiad — *the large cannon used to fire the projectile into space*

Answer these questions about the text that you've just read.
Circle the letter of the correct answer.

1. Which of these words is the closest in meaning to "fateful" (line 1)?

    A   Fortunate
    B   Terrible
    C   Significant
    D   Predictable
    E   Exciting

2. Why does the projectile need to be launched at a specific time?

    A   The needle of the chronometer has predicted the exact time to launch.
    B   This is the only moment for a long time with the exact conditions needed.
    C   Murchison thinks this is the best time for the launch.
    D   This is the time that everyone is ready to go.
    E   It is exactly eighteen years since they started working on the project.

Mixed Practice Tests

3. What does the phrase "charged with the duty" (line 6) mean?

   A   Accused of
   B   Given the job
   C   Released from
   D   Tempted by
   E   Confused by

4. "Even J. T. Maston had found in his own dry eyes one ancient tear" (lines 9-10). What impression does the reader get of J. T. Maston from these lines?

   A   He is very old.
   B   He doesn't know how to cry.
   C   He cries frequently.
   D   He doesn't often show emotion.
   E   He has problems with his eyes.

5. "A terrible silence weighed upon the entire scene." (line 12). What does this mean?

   A   Everyone has been told to be quiet.
   B   The projectile is very heavy.
   C   Something has gone horribly wrong.
   D   The silence feels tense.
   E   Everyone is desperate to say something.

6. "It wanted scarce forty seconds to the moment of departure" (line 15). What does this mean?

   A   It was only forty seconds until the projectile launched.
   B   The projectile launched forty seconds late.
   C   The projectile launched forty seconds early.
   D   It would take Murchison forty seconds to launch the projectile.
   E   It only took forty seconds for the projectile to launch.

7. What type of word is "departure" (line 8)?

   A   Adverb
   B   Adjective
   C   Common noun
   D   Verb
   E   Determiner

8. According to the passage, which of these statements is false?

   A   The travellers take their place in the projectile at 40 seconds past 10.48 pm.
   B   The travellers are going to be fired out of a large cannon.
   C   There are many people watching.
   D   The travellers are inside the projectile when Murchison discharges the spark.
   E   The projectile is being launched in December.

Mixed Practice Tests

> In this passage, there are some spelling mistakes. Circle the letter which matches the part of the sentence with the mistake. If there's no mistake, circle N.

9. Many people have unnusual talents, / but perhaps one / of the most extraordinary / is sword
   A / B / C / D / N

10. swallowing. / This seemingly impossible skill / involves a performer / passing a blade down
    A / B / C / D / N

11. their throat / and into their stomach. / The art of sword swallowing / has been practiced for
    A / B / C / D / N

12. thousands of years / by fearless entertainers / who posess steady hands / and nerves of steel.
    A / B / C / D / N

13. Obviously, / this skill is incredibley / dangerous and should / never be attempted at home!
    A / B / C / D / N

> Choose the right words or phrases to complete the passage. Circle the letter which matches the correct word.

14. These days **about almost above near close** every household owns at least one mirror.
    A   B   C   D   E

15. However, during the 16th century, mirrors **are were being be should be**
    A   B   C   D   E

16. incredibly precious and **most alone still few only** the very wealthy had one.
    A   B   C   D   E

17. The reason mirrors were so valuable was **due because why so whereas** only a handful
    A   B   C   D   E

18. of mirror makers **know knows known knew knowing** how to craft them.
    A   B   C   D   E

Total (out of 18):

CGP

> There are **multiple-choice answer sheets** for these questions on our website — go to www.cgpbooks.co.uk/11plusanswersheets. If you want to attempt each paper more than once, you will need to print a separate answer sheet for each attempt.

11+ English

For Ages 10-11
Practice Paper 1

For GL Assessment

Read the following:

Do not start the test until you are told to do so.

1. This is a multiple-choice test.

2. There are 50 questions and you will have 50 minutes to do the test.

3. You should mark your answer to each question in pencil on the answer sheet you've printed from www.cgpbooks.co.uk/11plusanswersheets.

4. You should only mark one answer for each question. To mark your answer, draw a straight line through the rectangle next to the option you have chosen. If you make a mistake, rub it out and mark your new answer clearly.

5. Make sure you keep your place on the answer sheet and mark your answer in the box that has the same number as the question.

6. Do as many questions as you can. If you get stuck on a question, choose the answer that you think is most likely to be correct, then move on to the next question.

7. You should do any rough working on a separate piece of paper.

Work carefully, but go as quickly as you can.

Practice Paper 1

Read this passage carefully and answer the questions that follow.

An adapted extract from 'Red Fox'
by Charles G. D. Roberts

One night, while the moonlight was yet bright on the glittering wilderness, the two foxes were playing together in the shining lane which the snow-covered channel of
5   the brook made through the forest. Their wounds had given little trouble to their hardy and healthy flesh. Their hunting had been good in the early part of the night. They were young, extremely well
10 satisfied with themselves and with each other; and the only occupation that met their mood was to chase each other round and round in short circles, leaping over each other's backs, and occasionally
15 grappling, rising on their hind legs, and biting at each other's throats with every pretence of ferocity. Unlike dogs, they made no noise in their play, except for the hushed rustle and patter of scurrying and
20 pushing feet, the occasional swish and crackle of the bushes they disturbed.

Suddenly, as they met after a circling rush, they checked themselves as they were just about to grapple, and stood
25 motionless, staring at a strange trail. It was the track of a man on snow-shoes. Their noses, anxiously inquiring, presently assured them that the trail was many hours old. Then they subjected
30 it to the most wondering and searching examination. Surely there could be no creature with such stupendous feet as that inhabiting their wilderness. But, if there were, they needed to find out all about it,
35 the more securely to avoid encountering such a monster.

About these great tracks, and especially near the centre of each, where the depression was deepest, there clung
40 the strong man scent, which puzzled them the more as they knew that the feet of man made no such prints. Then Red Fox identified the scent still more exactly, recognising it as that of his greatest foe,
45 the dreaded dispenser of fire and noise and death, Jabe Smith — the farmer. Upon this he came to realize that the gigantic tracks were made by something attached to Jabe Smith's feet. For what
50 purpose, or to what use, the man should so enlarge his feet Red Fox could not conceive; but he knew that men were always mysterious, and he was content to let the question go at that. The point
55 that interested both the foxes now was, to where did the tracks lead? What was the man's business here in their woods?

All thought of play laid aside, they now took up the trail, following cautiously, with
60 every sense on the alert. The trail led toward the farthest and wildest section of the she-fox's range. At length it came

Turn over to the next page

Practice Paper 1

to a halt, where it crossed a well-marked runway of her own. The snow was
65 trampled and disturbed at this point, and just here, where the runway was narrowed by a thick bush on either side, lay the frozen head and neck of a chicken. Red Fox, for all his natural wariness, was
70 starting forward to investigate this prize; but his mate, who had somehow obtained a certain knowledge of traps, thrust him aside so brusquely that he realized the presence of an unknown peril. Then, and
75 not till then, he noticed that at that point, around and beneath the chicken head, there were no fox tracks visible. They had evidently been covered with snow.

While he was considering this ominous
80 fact, his mate moved forward with the extreme of caution, sniffing at the snow before every step. With intense interest he watched her, realising that she knew something of which he, for all his craft,
85 was ignorant. In a moment or two she stopped, and began sniffing around the point at which she had stopped. The care she displayed in this amounted to timidity, and convinced Red Fox that something
90 terribly dangerous lay hidden beneath the snow. In a moment or two the prudent investigator began to dig, pawing away the snow with light, delicate, surface strokes; and presently she revealed a
95 small, dark, menacing thing, made of the same hard, cold substance which Red Fox had observed that so many of man's implements were made of. The snow on the middle of the trap the wise little
100 she-fox dared not disturb; and she flatly discouraged any very close examination on Red Fox's part. But she gave him to understand that this was one of the cunningest and most deadly of all the
105 devices which that incomprehensible creature, man, routinely employed against the wild creatures. And she also made him understand that unexpected blessings, like the chicken head, or other
110 unusual delicacies, when found scattered with seeming generosity about the forest ways, were pretty sure to indicate at least one trap in the immediate neighbourhood. Leaving the treacherous thing unmasked,
115 so that no other of the forest dwellers might be betrayed by it, the two foxes resumed the trapper's trail, to find out what more treasons he had plotted against the wild folk.
120 They had gone but a little way farther when a great noise of scrambling and struggling, just ahead, brought them to a sudden stop. It was a mysterious and daunting sound, as if some strong
125 creatures were fighting, voicelessly. With the utmost stealth they crept forward, along the snow-shoe trail, and came suddenly upon a terrifying spectacle.

Answer these questions about the text. You can refer back to the text if you need to.
Pick the best answer and mark its letter on your answer sheet.

1 According to the text, which of these statements is true?
- A   It is a dark night in the forest.
- B   The foxes are hungry.
- C   The foxes have fallen out with each other.
- D   The foxes are energetic.
- E   The foxes are in pain.

2 Chasing each other was "the only occupation that met their mood" (lines 11-12). What does this mean?
- A   It was the only thing that could cheer the foxes up.
- B   It was the only thing the foxes wanted to do.
- C   The foxes consider playing to be the most important thing.
- D   The foxes always play together at this time of night.
- E   It was the only thing that put the foxes in a bad mood.

3 The foxes "checked themselves as they were just about to grapple" (lines 23-24). Why do you think the author included this detail?
- A   To show that the foxes want to look at each other.
- B   To show that the foxes have run out of energy.
- C   To show that the foxes take potential danger seriously.
- D   To show that the foxes don't enjoy grappling each other.
- E   To show that the foxes don't want to hurt each other.

4 Which adjective best describes how the foxes feel about the track after they realise it is "many hours old" (line 29)?
- A   Distressed
- B   Nervous
- C   Frightened
- D   Excited
- E   Intrigued

5 What do the foxes initially think the tracks belong to?
- A   A monster
- B   A giant
- C   A dog
- D   A fox
- E   Jabe Smith

Turn over to the next page

Practice Paper 1

6 What do you think Red Fox means when he describes Jabe Smith as a "dispenser of fire and noise and death" (lines 45-46)?

- A Jabe Smith has set the forest on fire.
- B Jabe Smith's farm is very noisy.
- C Jabe Smith shoots and kills wild animals.
- D Jabe Smith makes a lot of noise when he walks through the forest.
- E Jabe Smith is hurting his farm animals.

7 According to the passage, which statement about Red Fox is false?

- A He sees Jabe Smith as his enemy.
- B He doesn't understand why Jabe Smith wears snow-shoes.
- C He finds humans hard to understand.
- D He wants to find out more about why men enlarge their feet.
- E He wants to know why Jabe Smith was in the forest.

8 The trail that the foxes follow leads to:

- A the farm where Jabe Smith lives.
- B a chicken run.
- C the outskirts of the forest.
- D a place where Red Fox has been before.
- E a place where the she-fox has been before.

9 Why do you think Red Fox starts to "investigate this prize" (line 70)?

- A He thinks it's a trap.
- B He's naturally inquisitive.
- C He wants to eat it.
- D The she-fox wants him to find out what it is.
- E He's naturally careful.

10 The she-fox pushes Red Fox "brusquely" (line 73). What does this suggest about her actions?

- A She is warning Red Fox.
- B She wants to hurt Red Fox.
- C She is being playful with Red Fox.
- D She wants to set off the trap.
- E She wants to get to the chicken head before Red Fox.

11 Why is it "ominous" (line 79) that no fox tracks were visible near the chicken head?

    A It shows that someone else is in the forest.
    B It shows that another animal has tried to disguise its tracks.
    C It shows that someone has tried to trick the foxes.
    D It shows that the chicken has been killed.
    E It shows that the foxes are in danger of getting lost.

12 Red Fox is described as "ignorant" (line 85) because:

    A he likes investigating things.
    B the she-fox knows something that he does not.
    C the she-fox is ignoring him.
    D he doesn't know anything about life in the forest.
    E he's in danger.

13 Why does the she-fox dig with "light, delicate, surface strokes" (lines 93-94)?

    A She isn't very strong.
    B She doesn't want Red Fox to see what she's doing.
    C She's being careful.
    D She doesn't want Jabe Smith to hear her digging.
    E The snow is difficult to dig.

14 What happens after the she-fox reveals the trap?

    A Red Fox examines it closely.
    B The she-fox examines it closely.
    C The she-fox clears the rest of the snow off it.
    D The foxes dig up another trap.
    E The she-fox stops Red Fox from studying it.

Turn over to the next page

15 What lesson does the she-fox teach Red Fox?

  A He shouldn't trust humans.
  B He should be afraid of chickens.
  C He should be wary of food left lying around in the forest.
  D He shouldn't eat anything in the forest.
  E He shouldn't eat chickens.

16 Why do the foxes leave "the treacherous thing unmasked" (line 114)?

  A To protect other animals
  B So that they could find it again
  C So that they wouldn't step in it on their way back.
  D To show Jabe Smith they had found it
  E To stop humans stepping in it

17 After the foxes leave the site of the trap, they:

  A betray the other forest dwellers.
  B try to find more traps.
  C go back home.
  D go to warn other creatures about the trap.
  E plot against Jabe Smith.

18 Why do you think the foxes creep with "the utmost stealth" (line 126)?

  A They are trying to avoid stepping in traps.
  B They don't want to disturb any other animals.
  C They think there could be something dangerous ahead.
  D They don't want to leave tracks in the snow.
  E They can see Jabe Smith ahead.

Practice Paper 1

Answer these questions about the meaning of words as they are used in the text.

19 Which of these phrases is closest in meaning to "stupendous" (line 32)?

- **A** Frightening and imposing
- **B** Ridiculous-looking
- **C** Intriguing-looking
- **D** Astonishingly large
- **E** Monstrous and grotesque

20 The word "obtained" (line 71) could most accurately be replaced by:

- **A** invented.
- **B** received.
- **C** stolen.
- **D** discovered.
- **E** gained.

21 The word "timidity" (line 88) could be most accurately be replaced by:

- **A** curiosity.
- **B** enthusiasm.
- **C** fear.
- **D** cowardice.
- **E** intensity.

22 Which of these is closest in meaning to "daunting" (line 124)?

- **A** Baffling
- **B** Intimidating
- **C** Unexpected
- **D** Strange
- **E** Intriguing

Turn over to the next page

Answer these questions about the way words and phrases are used in the text.

23 Which of the following phrases contains onomatopoeia?

A "leaping over each other's backs"
B "the occasional swish and crackle of the bushes"
C "the dreaded dispenser of fire and noise and death"
D "the cunningest and most deadly of all the devices"
E "a great noise of scrambling and struggling"

24 What type of words are these examples of?

subjected   conceive   discouraged   crept

A Adjectives
B Prepositions
C Conjunctions
D Verbs
E Adverbs

25 What type of word is "wariness" (line 69)?

A Common noun
B Pronoun
C Adjective
D Collective noun
E Verb

26 The phrase "the two foxes resumed the trapper's trail" (lines 116-117) contains an example of:

A an abbreviation.
B alliteration.
C an analogy.
D onomatopoeia.
E a simile.

Practice Paper 1

Beach Café Opening Soon

27 Sunny afternoons on East Beach are about to receive an upgrade with the imminent

28 arrival of a luxurius new café. The brainchild of local entrepreneur Hattie Rivers,

29 the café will throw open its doors to custommers within the next fortnight. Topping the

30 menu will be a range of sumtuous ice-cream innovations that Hattie hopes will become

31 legendery throughout the region — expect cream, nuts and plenty of chocolate syrup!

32 For those desiring something heartier, Hattie has devised a wierd and wonderful mix

33 of inventive meals. The vegetarien sausage rolls (made with lentils and tofu) are sure

34 to attract plenty of admirers, but I'll be heading strait for a buffalo and banana burger.

This passage contains some mistakes involving capital letters and punctuation. Each numbered line has either one mistake or no mistake. For each line, work out which group of words contains a mistake and mark the letter on your answer sheet. Mark N if there is no mistake.

Granny's Games

Dear Auntie Meena,

35 You're not going to believe this, but its happened again. I'm feeling queasy just thinking
    A   **B**   **C**   **D**   **N**

36 about it she's so embarrassing! There I was, sitting on my usual bench (the one near
    A   **B**   **C**   **D**   **N**

37 the lake) waiting for Lily and Rose to arrive. The park was deserted except for a family
        A   **B**   **C**   **D**   **N**

38 and dr Mellor, whose daughters are in my ice-skating class. I was excited to see Lily —
            A   **B**   **C**   **D**   **N**

39 she's been abroad for ages because of her mum's job. Approaching footsteps, made
        A   **B**   **C**   **D**   **N**

40 the geese on the lake scatter into the sky. I looked up, expecting to see my friend's faces.
            A   **B**   **C**   **D**   **N**

41 "Sunita! So good to see you! It wasn't Lily's voice though. It was Granny's. Why does
        A   **B**   **C**   **D**   **N**

42 she keep appearing like this, and why does she insist on wearing that tiger costume.
            A   **B**   **C**   **D**   **N**

Anyway, I hope you're well.

Love from Sunita.

Practice Paper 1

For each numbered line, choose the word, or group of words, which completes the passage correctly. The passage needs to make sense and be written in correct English. Pick one of the five options and mark the letter on your answer sheet.

Which Village will be Victorious?

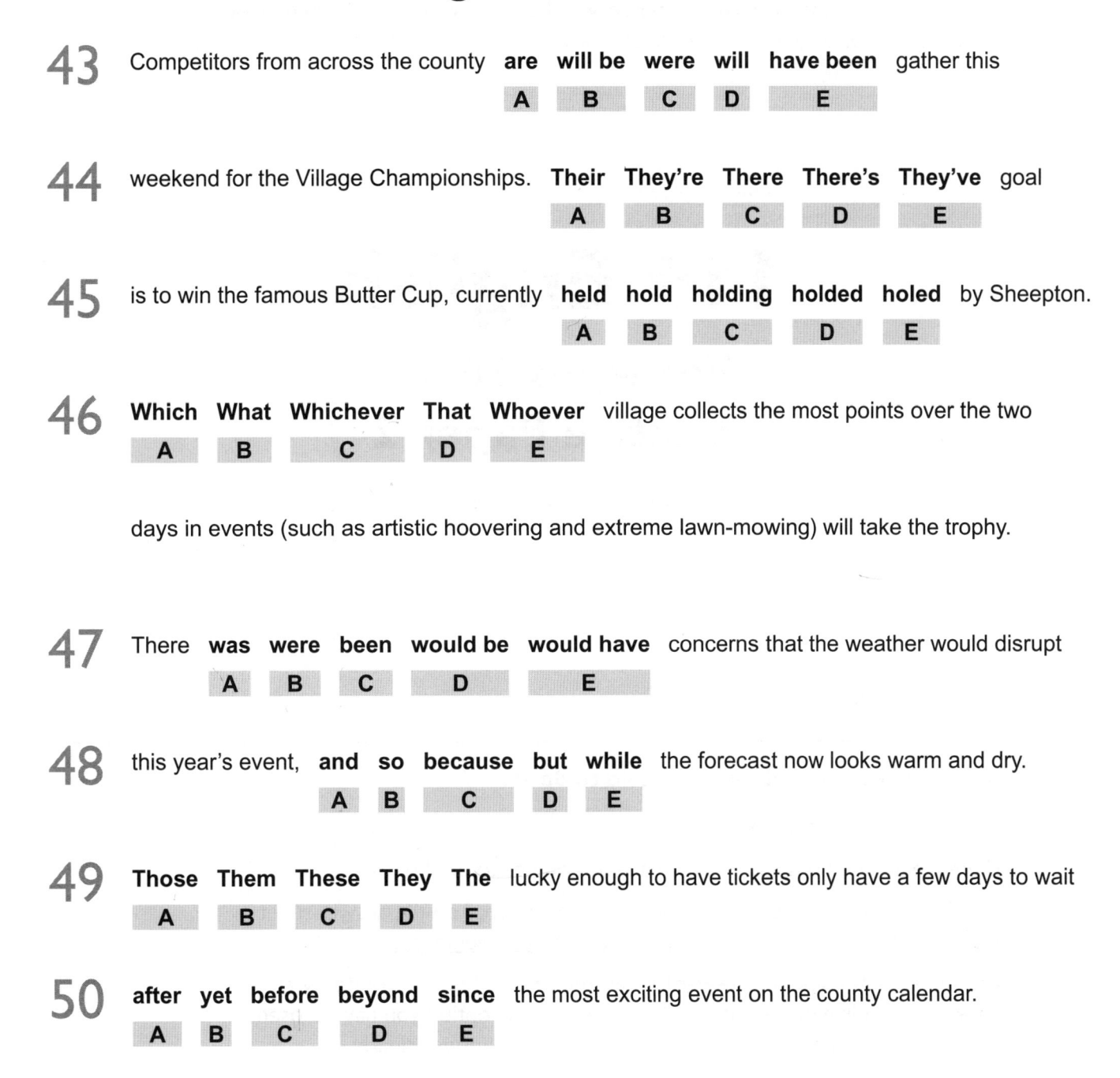

43 Competitors from across the county **are (A) will be (B) were (C) will (D) have been (E)** gather this

44 weekend for the Village Championships. **Their (A) They're (B) There (C) There's (D) They've (E)** goal

45 is to win the famous Butter Cup, currently **held (A) hold (B) holding (C) holded (D) holed (E)** by Sheepton.

46 **Which (A) What (B) Whichever (C) That (D) Whoever (E)** village collects the most points over the two

days in events (such as artistic hoovering and extreme lawn-mowing) will take the trophy.

47 There **was (A) were (B) been (C) would be (D) would have (E)** concerns that the weather would disrupt

48 this year's event, **and (A) so (B) because (C) but (D) while (E)** the forecast now looks warm and dry.

49 **Those (A) Them (B) These (C) They (D) The (E)** lucky enough to have tickets only have a few days to wait

50 **after (A) yet (B) before (C) beyond (D) since (E)** the most exciting event on the county calendar.

End of test

Practice Paper 1

CGP

> There are **multiple-choice answer sheets** for these questions on our website — go to www.cgpbooks.co.uk/11plusanswersheets. If you want to attempt each paper more than once, you will need to print a separate answer sheet for each attempt.

11+ English

For Ages 10-11
Practice Paper 2

For GL Assessment

Read the following:

Do not start the test until you are told to do so.

1. This is a multiple-choice test.

2. There are 50 questions and you will have 50 minutes to do the test.

3. You should mark your answer to each question in pencil on the answer sheet you've printed from www.cgpbooks.co.uk/11plusanswersheets.

4. You should only mark one answer for each question. To mark your answer, draw a straight line through the rectangle next to the option you have chosen. If you make a mistake, rub it out and mark your new answer clearly.

5. Make sure you keep your place on the answer sheet and mark your answer in the box that has the same number as the question.

6. Do as many questions as you can. If you get stuck on a question, choose the answer that you think is most likely to be correct, then move on to the next question.

7. You should do any rough working on a separate piece of paper.

Work carefully, but go as quickly as you can.

Practice Paper 2

Read this passage carefully and answer the questions that follow.

An adapted extract from 'The Yosemite'
by John Muir

When I set out on the long excursion that finally led to California, I wandered afoot and alone from Indiana to the Gulf of Mexico. I took a generally southward
5 course, like the birds when they are going from summer to winter. From the west coast of Florida I crossed the gulf to Cuba, intending to go on to the north end of South America, make my way through the
10 woods to the Amazon, and float down that grand river to the ocean. But I was unable to find a ship bound for South America — fortunately perhaps, for I had incredibly little money for so long a trip and had not
15 yet fully recovered from a fever caught in the Florida swamps. Therefore I decided to visit California for a year or two to see its wonderful flora and the famous Yosemite Valley.

20 On the first of April, 1868, I set out afoot for Yosemite. It was the bloom-time of the year and the landscapes of the Santa Clara Valley were fairly drenched with sunshine. The air was quivering with
25 the songs of the meadow-larks, and the hills were so covered with flowers that they seemed to be painted. Slow indeed was my progress through these glorious gardens. Cattle and cultivation were
30 making few scars as yet, and I wandered enchanted in long wavering curves, knowing by my pocket map that Yosemite Valley lay to the east and that I should surely find it.

*****

35 Situated in the basin of the Merced River at an elevation of 4000 feet above the level of the sea, the Yosemite Valley is about seven miles long and nearly a mile wide. The walls are made up of rocks,
40 mountains in size, partly separated from each other by side canyons. They are so sheer in front, and so compactly and harmoniously arranged on a level floor, that the Valley looks like an immense hall
45 or temple lighted from above.

But no temple made with hands can compare with Yosemite. Every rock in its walls seems to glow with life. Some lean back in majestic repose; others advance
50 beyond their companions in thoughtful attitudes, giving welcome to storms and calms alike. They have their feet among beautiful meadows, a thousand flowers leaning confidingly against them,
55 bathed in floods of water. Myriads of small winged creatures — birds, bees, butterflies — give glad animation and help to make all the air into music. Down through the middle of the Valley flows the
60 crystal Merced, peacefully quiet, reflecting lilies and trees and the onlooking rocks. It is as if into this one mountain mansion Nature has gathered her choicest treasures.

Turn over to the next page

Practice Paper 2

Answer these questions about the text. You can refer back to the text if you need to.
Pick the best answer and mark its letter on your answer sheet.

1 Which of these places does the narrator not travel to?

A Florida
B The Santa Clara Valley
C The Amazon
D Cuba
E Indiana

2 What causes the narrator's travel plans to change?

A The narrator doesn't have enough money.
B The narrator hears about the famous Yosemite Valley.
C The narrator catches a fever.
D The narrator changes his mind about where he wants to go.
E There isn't a boat to where the narrator wants to go.

3 The passage says that the Santa Clara Valley was "fairly drenched with sunshine" (lines 23-24). What does this image tell the reader?

A It was fairly sunny in the valley.
B It was very bright in the valley.
C It rained a lot as well as being sunny in the valley.
D It was very warm and humid in the valley.
E It had rained earlier but now the sun was out.

4 What do you think the narrator means by "the hills were so covered with flowers that they seemed to be painted" (lines 25-27)?

A It's impossible to tell there are flowers on the hills.
B The hills all appear to be the same colour.
C The flowers are ruining the natural beauty of the hills.
D The hills are covered with colourful flowers.
E People paint pictures of all the flowers on the hills.

5 According to the text, where is the Santa Clara Valley in relation to the Yosemite Valley?

A The Santa Clara Valley is to the north of the Yosemite Valley.
B The Santa Clara Valley is to the south of the Yosemite Valley.
C The Santa Clara Valley is to the east of the Yosemite Valley.
D The Santa Clara Valley is to the west of the Yosemite Valley.
E The narrator isn't sure.

Practice Paper 2

6 Which of these does the narrator not say about the valley in lines 39-45?

  A The walls are all part of one big mountain.
  B The walls are very steep.
  C It looks like an enormous building.
  D The bottom of the canyon is flat.
  E The walls are arranged neatly.

7 "But no temple made with hands can compare with Yosemite" (lines 46-47).
Why do you think the narrator says this?

  A The narrator thinks that humans aren't very good at building temples.
  B Yosemite is more ornate than any man-made temple.
  C Yosemite has better lighting than a man-made temple.
  D The narrator has seen man-made temples that are more beautiful than Yosemite.
  E The narrator thinks Yosemite is more impressive than any man-made temple.

8 The phrase "give glad animation" (line 57) shows that the narrator thinks that the birds and insects in Yosemite:

  A seem very happy.
  B look like cartoons.
  C make too much noise.
  D create a lively atmosphere.
  E bring joy to people who see them.

Answer these questions about meaning of words as they are used in the text.

9 The word "cultivation" (line 29) could most accurately be replaced by:

  A foraging.
  B farming.
  C construction.
  D transportation.
  E hunting.

10 Which of these words is closest in meaning to "choicest" (line 63)?

  A Prime
  B Rare
  C Familiar
  D Largest
  E Luminous

Turn over to the next page

Practice Paper 2

Answer these questions about the way words and phrases are used in the text.

11 "Slow indeed was my progress through these glorious gardens" (lines 27-29). The word "progress" is an example of what type of word?

- A Verb
- B Common noun
- C Adverb
- D Proper noun
- E Adjective

12 The word "alone" (line 3) is an example of which type of word?

- A Adjective
- B Pronoun
- C Common noun
- D Collective noun
- E Adverb

13 The passage says that some rocks "advance beyond their companions in thoughtful attitudes" (lines 49-51). What is this an example of?

- A A simile
- B An analogy
- C Personification
- D Onomatopoeia
- E Alliteration

Read this passage carefully and answer the questions that follow.

An adapted extract from 'The Butterfly's Dream'
by Hannah F. Gould

A tulip, just opened, had offered to hold
   A butterfly, gaudy and gay;
And, rocked in a cradle of crimson and gold,
   The careless young slumberer lay.

5   For the butterfly slept, as such thoughtless ones will,
     At ease, and reclining on flowers,
If ever they study, it is how they may kill
     The best of their mid-summer hours.

   And the butterfly dreamed, as is often the case
10   With *indolent* lovers of change,
Who, keeping the body at ease in its place,
     Give fancy permission to range.

He dreamed that he saw, what he could but despise,
     The swarm from a neighbouring hive;
15 Which, having come out for their winter supplies,
     Had made the whole garden alive.

He looked with disgust, as the proud often do,
     On the diligent movements of those,
Who, keeping both present and future in view,
20   Improve every hour as it goes.

As the brisk little honeybees passed to and fro,
     With anger the butterfly swelled;
And called them unworthy – a rabble too low
     To come near the station he held.

25 'Away from my presence!' said he, in his sleep,
     'Ye humble low peasants! Nor dare
Come here with your colourless winglets to sweep
     The king of this flowerbed fair!'

He thought, at these words, that together they flew,
30   And, facing about, made a stand;
And then, to a terrible army they grew,
     And fenced him on every hand.

Their eyes seemed like little volcanoes, for fire,—
     Their hum, to a cannon-peal grown,—
35 Fine pollen to bullets was rolled in their ire,
     And, he thought, hurled at him and his throne.

He tried to cry quarter! His voice would not sound,
     His head ached — his throne reeled and fell;
His enemy cheered, as he came to the ground,
40   And cried, 'King Papilio*, farewell!'

His fall chased the vision — the sleeper awoke,
     The wonderful dream was no more;
The lightning's bright flash from the
                        thunder-cloud broke,
And hail-stones were rattling the floor.

*Papilio — *the Latin word for 'butterfly'*

Turn over to the next page

Practice Paper 2

Answer these questions about the text. You can refer back to the text if you need to.
Pick the best answer and mark its letter on your answer sheet.

14 Which adjective best describes the tulip at the start of the poem?
   A   Peaceful
   B   Contemplative
   C   Unstable
   D   Carefree
   E   Welcoming

15 What does the poet mean by "Give fancy permission to range" (line 12)?
   A   The butterfly is allowed to be extravagant.
   B   The butterfly is given permission to imagine a variety of things.
   C   The butterfly's imagination is free to wander.
   D   The butterfly gives others permission to fantasise.
   E   The butterfly is free to go wherever he wants.

16 In the butterfly's dream, he sees "what he could but despise" (line 13). What does this mean?
   A   He sees the only thing that he dislikes.
   B   He sees something that he likes.
   C   He can't work out what he's seeing.
   D   He sees something he can't help disliking.
   E   He hates everything that he sees.

17 Why do the bees come into the garden?
   A   To collect food for winter
   B   To attack the butterfly
   C   To feed, because they're hungry
   D   To sleep on the flowers
   E   To raid a neighbouring hive

18 Why is the butterfly angry with the bees in verse 6?
   A   He thinks that they are moving too fast.
   B   They have made him swell up.
   C   The noise they are making has woken him up.
   D   They haven't asked his permission to approach him.
   E   He thinks that they aren't important enough to approach him.

Practice Paper 2

19 "And then, to a terrible army they grew, / And fenced him on every hand" (lines 31-32). Why do you think the poet uses the word "fenced" here?

- **A** The bees are attacking the butterfly with swords.
- **B** The bees have caused the butterfly offence.
- **C** The bees have encircled the butterfly.
- **D** The bees are attacking the butterfly with pieces of wood.
- **E** The bees have built a fence around the butterfly.

20 What does the butterfly think the bees sound like in verse 9?

- **A** Volcanoes erupting
- **B** A clap of thunder
- **C** A bell ringing
- **D** A quiet hum
- **E** A cannon being fired

21 What happens in verse 10 of the poem?

- **A** The butterfly shouts at the bees and the bees leave.
- **B** The butterfly wakes up as the bees say goodbye.
- **C** The butterfly feels ill and falls to the floor.
- **D** The bees cheer as they make the butterfly their king.
- **E** The bees leave because they've hurt the butterfly.

Answer these questions about the way words and phrases are used in the text.

22 What type of word is "unworthy" (line 23)?

- **A** Proper noun
- **B** Adverb
- **C** Preposition
- **D** Adjective
- **E** Abstract noun

23 "Their eyes seemed like little volcanoes" (line 33) is an example of:

- **A** onomatopoeia.
- **B** a simile.
- **C** an antonym.
- **D** a metaphor.
- **E** an abbreviation.

Turn over to the next page

Practice Paper 2

Answer these questions about the meaning of words as they are used in the text.

24 Which of these words is closest in meaning to "diligent" (line 18)?

- A Hasty
- B Abhorrent
- C Laborious
- D Conscientious
- E Nimble

25 Which of these words is closest in meaning to "ire" (line 35)?

- A Malice
- B Disquiet
- C Impatience
- D Dissatisfaction
- E Fury

26 The word "reeled" (line 38) could most accurately be replaced by:

- A disintegrated.
- B swayed.
- C ruptured.
- D twirled.
- E danced.

Practice Paper 2

This passage contains some spelling mistakes. Each numbered line has either one mistake or no mistake. For each line, work out which group of words contains a mistake, and mark the letter on your answer sheet. Mark N if there is no mistake.

The Rogue Robot

27 Amelia peered hopefully through the conservatry window. Eight hours had elapsed
    A / B / C / D / N

28 since she'd last layed eyes on Rod, but she was convinced he was still in the vicinity
    A / B / C / D / N

29 — in her experience, robots didn't just wander off. The garden was desserted though,
    A / B / C / D / N

30 so she trudged back into the kitchen to seek solace in a chocolate digestive. Tim, her
    A / B / C / D / N

31 nuisance of a brother, had a theory that Rod had climed over the fence to initiate a
    A / B / C / D / N

32 malicious plan to terrorise the neighbour's gooses, but that was utter nonsense. Even
    A / B / C / D / N

33 if Rod had malfunctioned, there wasn't a sinister screw in his sleek metalic body, was
    A / B / C / D / N

34 there? Doubt siezed Amelia and she couldn't extinguish the thoughts that troubled her.
    A / B / C / D / N

Turn over to the next page

Practice Paper 2

This passage contains some mistakes involving capital letters and punctuation. Each numbered line has either one mistake or no mistake. For each line, work out which group of words contains a mistake and mark the letter on your answer sheet. Mark N if there is no mistake.

Sheds For Sale

35 Do you need some more peace, and quiet in your life? Are you fed up with your family?
    A   B   C   D   N

36 If so, it's time to consider how a new shed could help you. Sharon's sheds (located on
    A   B   C   D   N

37 Fountain Avenue) has been a world leading provider of top-quality sheds for over fifty
    A   B   C   D   N

38 years, with customer's including the actor Phil Man, athlete Izzy Quick and local MP
    A   B   C   D   N

39 Noah Clew. Sheds are a perfect place to escape life's: noise, stress and distractions —
    A   B   C   D   N

40 they're your very own space to relax. You can even plant a few seeds while you're at it.
    A   B   C   D   N

41 Still not convinced? Heres a testimonial from Linda Chen — one of our top customers:
    A   B   C   D   N

42 "My shed has changed my life, my husband's life and our sons' lives. It's truly amazing"!
    A   B   C   D   N

Practice Paper 2

For each numbered line, choose the word, or group of words, which completes the passage correctly. The passage needs to make sense and be written in correct English. Pick one of the five options and mark the letter on your answer sheet.

The Historic Tour

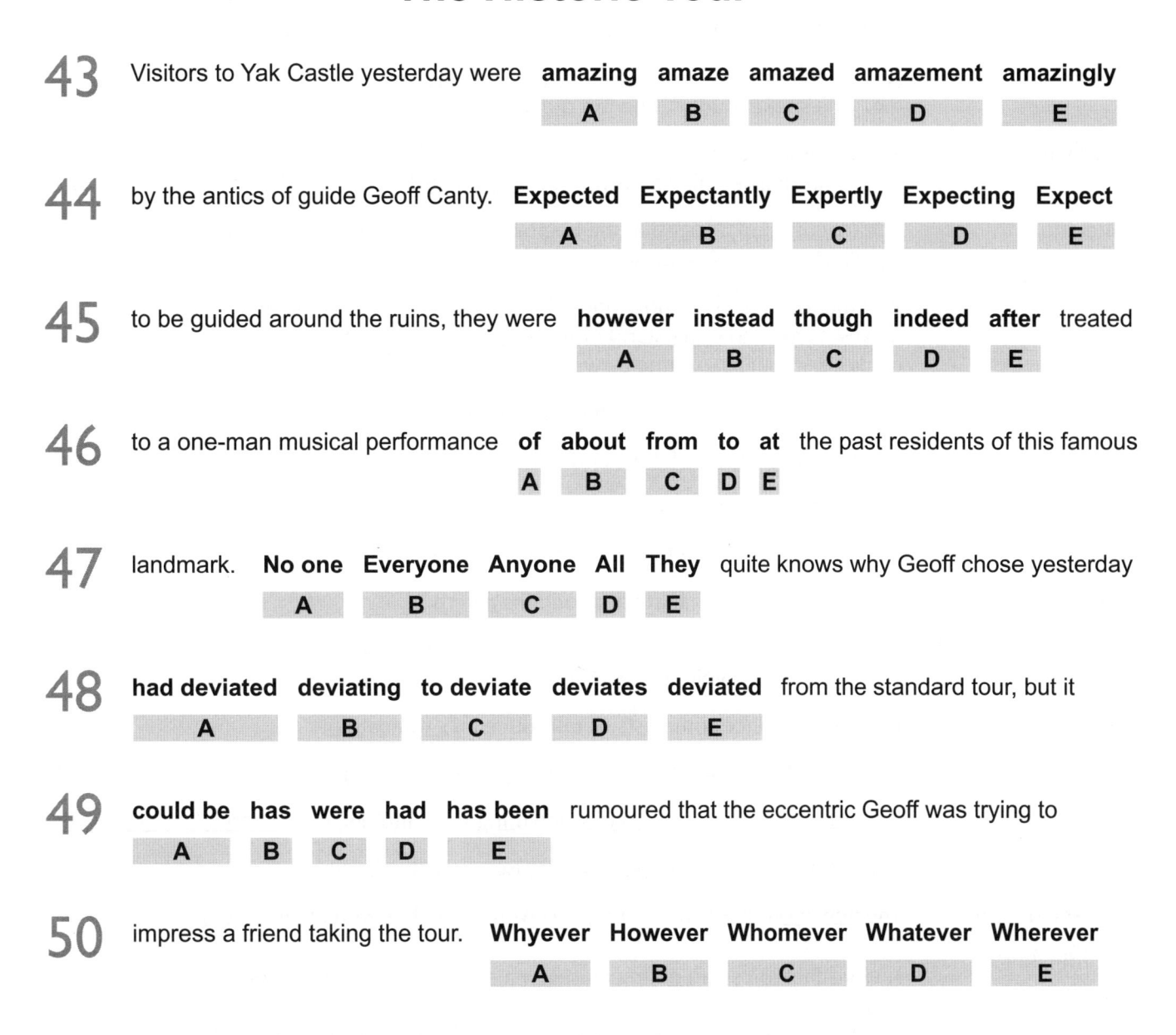

43 Visitors to Yak Castle yesterday were — A amazing / B amaze / C amazed / D amazement / E amazingly

44 by the antics of guide Geoff Canty. — A Expected / B Expectantly / C Expertly / D Expecting / E Expect

45 to be guided around the ruins, they were — A however / B instead / C though / D indeed / E after — treated

46 to a one-man musical performance — A of / B about / C from / D to / E at — the past residents of this famous

47 landmark. — A No one / B Everyone / C Anyone / D All / E They — quite knows why Geoff chose yesterday

48 A had deviated / B deviating / C to deviate / D deviates / E deviated — from the standard tour, but it

49 A could be / B has / C were / D had / E has been — rumoured that the eccentric Geoff was trying to

50 impress a friend taking the tour. — A Whyever / B However / C Whomever / D Whatever / E Wherever

the reason, he certainly gave one group of tourists a history lesson to remember!

End of test

Practice Paper 2

Glossary

abbreviation	A shortened version of a word, e.g. "bike" instead of "bicycle".
acronym	A word formed from the initial letters of a name or by combining initial letters of a series of words, e.g. "NATO" (North Atlantic Treaty Organisation).
adjective	A word that describes a noun, e.g. "beautiful morning", "frosty lawn".
adverb	A word that usually describes a verb or an adjective, e.g. "she spoke loudly", "he ran quickly".
adverbial	A word or group of words which acts like an adverb (it describes a verb), e.g. "Emir finished his homework before dinner."
alliteration	The repetition of a sound at the beginning of words within a phrase, e.g. "Loopy Lois likes lipstick."
analogy	A comparison to show how one thing is similar to another, which makes it easier to understand or remember. E.g. "watching cricket is about as exciting as watching paint dry."
antonym	A word that has the opposite meaning to another, e.g. "good" and "bad".
apostrophe	Used to show missing letters and belonging (possession).
article	The words 'the', 'a', or 'an' which go before a noun. A type of determiner.
brackets	Used to separate extra information in a sentence.
clause	A bit of a sentence that always contains a verb.
cliché	A phrase that has been overused and has lost some of its impact, e.g. "Avoid it like the plague."
colon	Used to introduce some lists or introduce an explanation.
comma	Separates items in a list and separates extra information.
comparative	A word or phrase that compares one thing with another, e.g. "shorter", "worse".
conjunction	A word or words used to link two clauses, e.g. "but", "since".
contracted form	The new word made by joining two words together with an apostrophe.
co-ordinating conjunction	A word that joins two main clauses in a sentence, e.g. "and", "or".
dash	Used to separate extra information in a sentence or join two main clauses together.
determiner	A word that goes before a noun to tell you whether it is general or specific.
direct speech	The actual words that are said by someone.
fiction	Text that has been made up by the author, about imaginary people and events.
homographs	Words that are spelt the same, but have different meanings, e.g. row (argue/paddle).
homophones	Words that sound the same, but mean different things, e.g. "hair" and "hare".
hyphen	Used to join words together to help avoid confusion, or to add a prefix to a word.
idiom	A phrase which doesn't literally mean what it says, e.g. "raining cats and dogs".
imagery	Language that creates a vivid picture in the reader's mind.

Glossary

initialism	An abbreviation that uses the first letters of words in a phrase, which are pronounced as separate letters. E.g. "PTO" = "please turn over".
irony	When a writer says the opposite of what they mean, or when the opposite happens to what the reader expects.
main clause	An important bit of a sentence that would make sense on its own, e.g. "They cleaned before they left." "They cleaned" is the main clause.
metaphor	A way of describing something by saying that it is something else, e.g. "John's legs were lead weights."
non-fiction	Text that is about facts and real people and events.
noun	A word that names something, e.g. "Paul", "scissors", "flock", "loyalty".
noun phrase	A group of words which includes a noun and any words that describe it, e.g. "Johan opened the heavy old door at the top of the stairs."
onomatopoeia	When words sound like the noise they describe, e.g. "pop", "bang", "squelch".
personification	A way of describing something by giving it human feelings and characteristics, e.g. "The cruel wind plucked remorselessly at my threadbare clothes."
phrase	A small part of a sentence, usually without a verb.
prefix	Letters that can be put in front of a word to change its meaning, e.g. "unlock".
preposition	A word that tells you how things are related, e.g. "in", "above", "before", "of".
pronoun	Words that can be used instead of nouns, e.g. "I", "you", "he", "it".
proverb	A short, commonly used phrase which usually gives a general truth or words of advice, e.g. "Don't count your chickens before they've hatched."
rhetorical question	A question that doesn't need an answer, e.g. "When will they learn?"
semicolon	Used to separate lists of longer things and to join sentences.
simile	A way of describing something by comparing it to something else, e.g. "The stars were like a thousand diamonds, glittering in the sky."
Standard English	English that uses correct grammar, spelling and punctuation.
subject	The person or thing doing the action of a verb, e.g. "Jo laughed", "the bird flew".
subjunctive form	A verb form that appears in formal writing, e.g. "If I were you, I would do it."
subordinate clause	A less important bit of a sentence which doesn't make sense on its own, e.g. "Although I ran, I was late." "Although I ran" is the subordinate clause.
subordinating conjunction	A word or group of words which joins a main clause to a subordinate clause, e.g. "even though", "because".
suffix	Letters that can be put after a word to change its meaning, e.g. "playful".
superlative	A word that refers to the most or least of a group of things, e.g. "the best team".
synonym	A word with a similar meaning to another word, e.g. "big" and "huge".
unstressed vowel	A vowel sound that is unclear, e.g. the "a" in "private".
verb	An action or being word, e.g. "I run", "he went", "you are", "we think".

Glossary

Answers

Section One — Grammar

Pages 4-6 — Nouns and Pronouns

1) a) 'swarm' is a collective noun.
    b) 'December' is a proper noun.
    c) 'Scotland' is a proper noun.
    d) 'cauliflower' is a common noun.
    e) 'lady' is a common noun.
    f) 'ostrich' is a common noun.
    g) 'class' is a collective noun.
    h) 'hockey' is a common noun.
    i) 'Sue' and 'Shaw' are both proper nouns.

Proper nouns are names; collective nouns are words for groups of things; common nouns are words for types of things.

2) Omaira and Yasmin swam desperately towards the island in the distance, although **it** wasn't getting any closer. After a while, **they** felt their feet touch the sandy shore and **they** knew that they had made it. Omaira looked around and **she** saw a completely deserted paradise which had never been visited by humans before. Yasmin saw a tree heavily laden with fruit a short distance away.
"Come on Omaira," **she** said. "Let's get something to eat."

The words in bold show where pronouns have replaced nouns.

Pages 7-9 — Verbs

1) a) The concert <u>starts</u> in ten minutes' time.
    b) We <u>finished</u> our fun run in record time, despite the bird costumes.
    c) Clotilde <u>perfected</u> the decorations on the birthday cake.
    d) I <u>love</u> rock-climbing in the Lake District during the summer.
    e) Christmas <u>brings</u> increased business to many toy shops.
    f) The steam train <u>rushes</u> past on its way to the coast.

The underlined words are the verbs — remember that verbs are action words or being words.

2) a) Barney has **eaten** all of my popcorn.
    b) I have **been** to South Africa on holiday.
    c) Hannah's knee is **hurting** after she fell over.
    d) You should **go** home or you'll be late.
    e) What time do you think you will **arrive**?
    f) The dolphin is about to **leap** out of the water.

Read the sentence out loud to help you find the right answer.

Pages 10-11 — Adjectives, Adverbs and Prepositions

1) a) 'funnier' is a comparative.
    b) 'strangest' is a superlative.
    c) 'most graceful' is a superlative.
    d) 'bizarre' is an adjective.
    e) 'joyful' is an adjective.
    f) 'less fascinating' is a comparative.

Comparatives often end in 'er' and superlatives often end in 'st'.

2) a) Chris closed his eyes <u>nervously</u> as the shuttle started to move. (adverb)
    b) Joyce leant over to tell Aniela to try the <u>crispy</u> beef. (adjective)
    c) Molly looked <u>around</u> the building, but she couldn't find anything. (preposition)
    d) I was the <u>only</u> child waiting to be collected after school. (adjective)
    e) Carrie <u>gladly</u> accepted the offer of a place to stay. (adverb)
    f) When Mum shouted, Terry always crawled <u>under</u> the table and sulked. (preposition)

The words in bold are the part of speech you need to identify.

Pages 12-13 — Determiners

1) a) **A** goat stole my snowboard.
    b) Ken put **our** muddy boots outside.
    c) Have you locked **their** garage?
    d) Liam ate **more** lollipops than you.

The words in bold are the determiners that complete each sentence.

2) Monty had been <u>a</u> farmer for <u>twenty</u> years. He'd spent <u>his</u> whole life in <u>the</u> small, remote village where he was born. <u>This</u> year, he was going to leave everything behind and move to <u>the</u> city.

The words that are underlined are the determiners.

Pages 14-17 — Sentences, Clauses and Phrases

1) a) <u>Before I go to bed</u>, I always brush my teeth.
   b) <u>Although he loves his job</u>, the gardener is retiring.
   c) Shakil can't go swimming <u>because he's got an upset stomach</u>.

The words that are underlined make up the subordinate clause.

2) a) complex sentence
   b) compound sentence
   c) compound sentence

Compound sentences contain clauses that each make sense on their own. Complex sentences contain clauses that don't make sense on their own.

Pages 18-19 — Conjunctions

1) The Amazon Rainforest covers 40% of South America, <u>although</u> it has decreased in size. Humans have cut down the trees <u>because</u> they need wood for construction <u>and</u> space for farms <u>and</u> roads. Conservation efforts are under way to protect the rainforest <u>and</u> stop people from illegally cutting down the trees.

The words that are underlined are the conjunctions.

2) a) I often eat cereal for breakfast **but** I sometimes eat toast.
   b) I'd like to go out to the Italian restaurant tonight, **although** Chinese is my favourite.

Look at the context to find the correct conjunction.

Pages 20-21 — Standard English and Formal Writing

1) a) Kyra <u>was</u> angry because Leo had lied to her.
   b) My dad was singing <u>badly</u> in the shower.
   c) "I think I <u>did</u> the right thing yesterday," said Marco.
   d) She doesn't like <u>those</u> sausage rolls.

The words that are underlined complete each sentence using Standard English.

2) a) Various answers possible, e.g. 'Have you spoken to Esme about the car's engine?'
   b) Various answers possible, e.g. 'If I were stronger, I would be able to lift the box.'
   c) Various answers possible, e.g. 'Berta thought it would be exciting, but it was not.'
   d) Various answers possible, e.g. 'He demands that she apologise immediately.'

Correct answers should avoid contracted forms. They might make use of the subjunctive form or more complicated words.

Pages 22-25 — Answering Grammar Questions

1) a) The conjunction is 'and'.
   b) 'desperate' is an adjective because it describes Harriet.
   c) 'angrily' is an adverb.

You'll need to think about the different parts of speech to identify the correct answer.

Pages 26-29 — Practice Questions

1) I lost my purse, but luckily Zac found <u>it</u>.
2) She had an argument with her parents and is refusing to speak to <u>them</u>.
3) We both made a salad — they loved his but they didn't like <u>mine</u>.
4) Charlie wanted to stroke the cat, but it hissed at <u>him</u>.
5) Ahil and I are going to the funfair — <u>we</u> are very excited.

Read the sentence carefully to work out what the pronoun refers to.

6) **go** — Mei suggested that we **go** to the cinema to watch that film.
7) **travelling** — They will be **travelling** around the world to mark their retirement.
8) **were** — Who **were** you talking to on the telephone earlier?
9) **remember** — I don't **remember** which school you went to.
10) **spotted** — We haven't **spotted** anything unusual in his behaviour so far.

Think about what tense the sentence is written in.

11) It was an <u>extremely</u> hot day, so we stayed at home. (adverb)
12) Sally was <u>overjoyed</u> at the news that she had won the competition. (adjective)
13) I looked <u>through</u> the window and saw them playing volleyball. (preposition)
14) Adam hopped over the gate and landed in a <u>deep</u> puddle. (adjective)
15) The poorly calf was feeding <u>well</u> after being reunited with its mother. (adverb)
16) Annoyingly, my train was delayed <u>by</u> a signal failure. (preposition)

The underlined words are the part of speech you need to identify.

17) <u>Those</u> horses can gallop faster than the others.
18) I would rather have an ice cream than <u>some</u> bitter lemonade.
19) Alisha couldn't believe <u>her</u> eyes when she saw a lion in the garden.

Answers

20) After the hike, <u>our</u> legs were aching a lot.
21) They had read <u>all</u> of the books in the small library.

Only one of the determiners makes sense in each sentence, so read the sentence carefully to work out which one fits.

22) <u>The people who live next door</u> play loud music all day. — **noun phrase**
23) Claudia is bored, so she wants to leave <u>tomorrow morning</u>. — **adverbial**
24) <u>The intrepid explorer</u> trekked deeper into the jungle. — **noun phrase**
25) She goes to the dentist <u>every six months</u>. — **adverbial**
26) <u>As quietly as possible</u>, I crept out from my hiding place. — **adverbial**
27) <u>A village close to Gloucester</u> has been without power for days. — **noun phrase**

An adverbial is a word or a group of words that behaves like an adverb. Noun phrases include a noun and any words describing the noun, including determiners, adjectives and preposition phrases.

28) Hasan made dinner <u>and</u> did the washing-up.
29) She kept thinking about <u>whether</u> he had lost his way.
30) Dylan was greeted warmly <u>although</u> he arrived very late.
31) It's a poor result <u>however</u> you look at it.
32) I discovered a pleasant path <u>while</u> I was out jogging.

Think carefully about which conjunction makes sense with the rest of the sentence.

33) He laughed really <u>noisily</u> in the playground.
34) They <u>were</u> thrilled about the result of the match.
35) <u>Those</u> cats are noisy, especially at night.
36) The apple <u>that</u> he ate was rotten.
37) She held the bird very <u>gently</u>.

Be careful — you've probably heard lots of people using non-Standard English before, so some of the wrong answers might sound familiar.

38) There were <u>more</u> unread books on his shelf than mine.
39) Naira was told off <u>whenever</u> she argued with her brother.
40) The fruit bowl was placed <u>on</u> the coffee table.
41) He asked me how I was but I did not know what to tell <u>him</u>.
42) I had <u>slept</u> for seven hours when I suddenly woke up.
43) I ate my dinner very <u>quickly</u>.

These questions test different grammar topics from this section.

Section Two — Punctuation

Pages 30-32 — Starting and Ending Sentences

1) a) Look out — it's the mutant cheesecake!
   b) Does this hat make my ears look funny?

You always begin a sentence with a capital letter, but you need to read the whole sentence before you know what to add to the end.

2) a) - d) Various answers possible.

Make sure you've used all the types of punctuation correctly.

3) 1 Peter Handy was a fisherman. Every day he went out on his boat in the bay to
   2 catch fish. One day he went down to the dock as usual to find his boat missing**.**
   3 "Oh dear!" cried Peter. "What am I going to do now**?**"
   4 He sat down on the dock and put his head in his hands. But just then**...**

Line 1 contains no errors. Line 2 needs a full stop at the end of the line after the word 'missing', whilst line 3 needs a question mark before the second set of inverted commas close. Line 4 ends on a cliffhanger, so an ellipsis should be used at the end of the line.

Pages 33-35 — Commas, Dashes and Brackets

1) a) Eddie**,** the newest addition to the family**,** was just three days old.
   b) Ravens**,** pigeons and seagulls were Nicci's least favourite types of bird.
   c) Although they couldn't hear**,** George shouted angrily at the boys as they ran away.

It can be tricky to add commas that separate different clauses — look out for where you need to pause so that the sentence makes sense.

2) **Ram and Lucy** were sick of their P.E. teacher**,** Mr Oden. Every day he made them do high jump, shot-put, **rugby and football**. One day they came up with a cunning plan (**along with the other children**) to get revenge on Mr Oden. They took all of the studs **out of** his football boots (**they stole them from under his desk**) so that when he put them on and started running**,** he fell head first into the mud.

There are 10 punctuation errors — make sure you've spotted them all and any new punctuation is in the right place.

Pages 36-37 — Apostrophes and Hyphens

1) a) Megan's goalkeeper jersey **wasn't** going to dry in time for her match.

Answers

b) "There's no way that you're going out when **it's** this cold," shouted Zac's mum.

c) Beatrice suddenly realised that she'd left her homework at her **dad's** house.

d) The **men's** boots were covered in mud from the garden.

Look out for clues in the sentence, like words ending in 's' that might show possession.

2) a) Needs a hyphen. The sentence should be 'Claudia bought an orange-striped teapot.'

b) Needs hyphens. The sentence should be 'The four-year-old children were playing in the sand.'

c) Needs a hyphen. The sentence should be 'The pile of well-folded clothes fell onto the floor.'

d) Doesn't need any hyphens.

Hyphens are usually used to clarify meaning in a phrase.

Pages 38-39 — Speech

1) a) "Listen carefully," said Matt, as he told them about the wizard's warning.

b) Alex screamed into the night air, "Why can't I find the way?"

c) "I need three starters, two desserts and one drink," shouted the waiter.

Inverted commas should only contain the words that are spoken.

2) a) "How many people are coming?" asked Giles.

b) Helen asked, "Will you have time to visit Maggie, Jurgen? I'm too busy."

c) "Take some sun cream!" shouted Heidi. "It's sweltering out there."

Whenever you add inverted commas to a sentence, think about where they should go in relation to the other punctuation.

Pages 40-41 — Colons and Semicolons

1) Pierre was very excited: it was the end of term. He was going to Greece on holiday the very next day. Pierre was looking forward to swimming in the bright blue **sea; browsing** the local Greek markets, looking for souvenirs; playing tennis at the **hotel; and** paying a visit to Athens. He didn't want to go to any **museums; his** mum would probably make him go anyway.

The first error is in the third sentence — a semicolon should be used instead of a colon to separate items in a list. The second error is at the end of the third sentence — there should be a semicolon before 'and'. The third error is in the final sentence — a semicolon should be used instead of a colon after 'museums' because the second clause does not explain what comes before it.

2) a) I've worked really hard; I expect to pass my exams.

b) I never miss a football match; I'm the top scorer in the team.

c) I went to the market for a new hat, but they didn't have any; I'll be back on Monday.

d) I would like to thank my mum, who inspired me to sing; my teacher, who taught me how to hit the high notes; and my partner, who wrote me some great songs.

Two semicolons should be added to the final sentence to separate the items in the list.

Pages 44-47 — Practice Questions

1) We are so excited to see you!

2) Giraffes have long necks to reach the highest leaves.

3) She was creeping past the entrance to the lair, when suddenly...

4) Where can we find a baker to make such a large pie?

5) Don't eat that — it's poisonous!

A full stops goes at the end of an ordinary sentence, an exclamation mark shows strong feelings or surprise, a question mark goes at the end of questions, and an ellipsis shows that a sentence is unfinished or was interrupted.

6) **incorrect** — The sentence should be: 'Lobsters, which have big claws, live on the ocean floor.'

7) **correct**

8) **incorrect** — The sentence should be: 'She relaxed into the comfortable armchair with a sigh.

9) **correct**

10) **incorrect** — The sentence should be: We bought a set of pencils, pens, a sharpener and a glue stick.

Commas can be used to separate items in a list. Commas can also be used to make meanings clearer and to separate fronted adverbials and subordinate clauses from the rest of a sentence.

11) Lancaster (a city in the north of England) has a medieval castle.

12) Ron (who speaks Italian) arranged the trip to Venice in the summer.

13) When they arrive (assuming they do) we'll ask why they're late.

14) Oliver and Laurissa (both sales assistants) took ballet classes.

15) The stories he told (there were many) fascinated the children.

Brackets, like pairs of commas or dashes, separate extra information from the rest of the sentence. The sentence should still make sense if you remove the bit in brackets.

Answers

16) **couldn't** — Jatin **couldn't** help us take care of the cats.
17) **won't** — He **won't** be able to come because he is ill.
18) **Daniel's** — **Daniel's** new ballet classes will start in two weeks.
19) **it's** — Thank you for hosting us all — **it's** been a pleasure.
20) **They're** — **They're** happy to discuss the changes to your plans.
21) **children's** — The **children's** toys broke when they fell off the table.

Apostrophes are used to show possession and in contracted forms of words.

22) Molly has a <u>ten-year-old snake</u> called Simon.
23) Lewis's <u>accident-prone sister</u> tripped over a branch.
24) This <u>state-of-the-art machine</u> will make our lives easier.
25) The scientists discovered a new species of <u>cave-dwelling bats</u>.
26) The <u>ever-more-exhausted</u> man climbed the hill slowly.
27) The <u>family-owned café</u> was established in 1975.

In these questions, only the words describing the noun should be hyphenated — the noun itself shouldn't be.

28) I politely asked**,** "Could you lend me your red pencil, please**?**"
29) Lily said**,** "Thank you for cooking my dinner**.**"
30) "Turn that music down now**!**" bellowed Anjali.
31) "She told me she wasn't coming**,**" replied Joey.
32) "Do you know what's happening over there**?**" Rob enquired.

Punctuation at the end of speech should be placed inside the inverted commas.

33) The carnival went down the street**;** the crowd was cheering wildly.
34) The kitchen was completely flooded**:** a water pipe had burst.
35) The acrobats performed their routine**;** the clowns waited in the wings.
36) These people need to see me**:** Hannah, Faisal and Luke.
37) This flight has been cancelled**;** ferries and train services are still running.

Colons are used to introduce lists and explanations. Semicolons join related clauses together and can also be used to break up lists.

38) I was surprised when (quite suddenly) a mouse appeared**)**.

The bracket after 'appeared' shouldn't be there. Brackets should only enclose extra information in a sentence.

39) Lionel declared<u>.</u> "This is the best play we've ever staged."

The full stop after 'declared' should be a comma. If there are words before the speech to introduce it, there should be a comma before the first set of inverted commas.

40) The town council <u>would'nt</u> listen to the residents' complaints.

The apostrophe should go between the 'n' and the 't' — it shows where the letter 'o' has been removed from the word 'not'.

41) I glued the vase back together<u>:</u> I hope they won't notice.

The colon should be a semicolon — the second clause doesn't explain the first, and the two clauses are equally important.

42) African elephants<u>;</u> which are the largest land mammals, live in herds.

The semicolon after 'elephants' should be a comma — the comma helps to separate the extra information from the sentence.

43) If there's a problem with your computer, try looking at <u>it's</u> settings.

Instead of 'it's', the word before 'settings' should be 'its'. 'It's' is a contracted form of 'it is' or 'it has', neither of which make sense in this sentence.

Section Three — Spelling

Pages 48-49 — Plurals

1) a) The plural of 'branch' is 'branches'.
   b) The plural of 'tooth' is 'teeth'.
   c) The plural of 'Grady' is 'Gradys'.
   d) The plural of 'daisy' is 'daisies'.
   e) The plural of 'dress' is 'dresses'.

Words ending with 'ch' or 's' usually take an 'es' plural, and words ending with 'y' usually take an 'ies' plural unless they are proper nouns.

Pages 50-51 — Homophones and Homographs

1) I'm supposed to go to drama group every Monday **night**, but this **week** I'm too tired. I've had a very busy day at school and I'm not feeling **great**. Instead, I think I'm going to stay **here** and watch a film that I haven't **seen** before.

The words in bold are the correct homophones.

2) a) Make sure that you know **where** you are going.
   b) Watch out for the crab — it has very sharp **claws**.
   c) At the theme park, we **rode** on four different roller coasters.
   d) The jockey pulled on the **reins** to get the horse to stop.

The correct answer should have a meaning which fits the context.

Pages 52-53 — Prefixes and Suffixes

1) a) The baby polar bear is so **adorable**.
   b) I was trying to be **helpful** when I washed the dishes.
   c) The ball hit Kayley and knocked her **unconscious**.
   d) Laszlo's feeling of **happiness** increased when he found his shoes.
   e) The apple was covered in mould and the flesh was **rotten**.

The prefix and suffixes which have been added all fit the context of the sentences.

Pages 54-55 — Silent Letters and Double Letters

1) a) I **maintained** a comfortable position for the whole journey.
   b) You need to wear more **clothes** in winter to keep warm.
   c) My **interesting** entry will win the competition tomorrow.

Make sure that double letters have been used correctly.

2) a) Everyone agreed that the charity event had been **successful**.
   b) While we're in London, we want to visit Nelson's **Column**.
   c) Sasha is the most **intelligent** girl in the class.
   d) I arrived just as the show was **beginning**.

These are the correct spellings of each word.

Pages 56-57 — Other Awkward Spellings

1) a) My car is running out of **diesel**.
   b) Don't forget to paint the **ceiling**.
   c) Adaliz's **height** has increased by 9 cm this year.
   d) Mr Harris went to the museum to see the **ancient** remains.

Use the rule "'i' before 'e' except after 'c', but only when it rhymes with bee" to help you to work out the correct spellings.

2) a) The missing letter is 'e' in 'desp**e**rate'.
   b) The missing letter is 'o' in 'fact**o**ry'.
   c) The missing letter is 'i' in 'respons**i**ble'.
   d) The missing letter is 'o' in 'harm**o**ny'.
   e) The missing letters are 'e' and 'a' in 'lit**e**r**a**ture'.
   f) The missing letter is 'a' in 'pass**a**ge'.

These are the vowels needed to correctly spell each word.

Pages 60-63 — Practice Questions

1) The **boys** had forgotten that they had a swimming lesson today.
2) All of the **marshes** around our house are full of wildlife.
3) Several **cities** wanted to host the Olympic Games.
4) Both **halves** of the pizza were delicious.
5) I don't have enough general knowledge to win many **quizzes.**

Lots of plurals are formed by adding 's', but some words follow different rules — make sure you know these trickier plurals.

6) A lot of waste ends up in landfill rather than being recycled.
7) Helena bought some leeks to have with dinner.
8) Eva told an exciting story about her adventure in outer space.
9) Several panes of glass had been smashed by debris during the storm.
10) The ball was thrown back over the fence by the friendly neighbour.
11) The farmers sow the fields with wheat and barley.

Homophones sound the same but have different meanings — look at the whole sentence to work out which one makes the most sense.

12) We apologised wholeheartedly for the **mis**understanding.
13) Everything they said about me was entire**ly** false.
14) Malik finds his employ**ment** in a supermarket very fulfilling.
15) A large van **trans**ports vegetables from our farm to a local restaurant.
16) All of the lights in our house stopped working, so we called an electri**cian**.
17) Gemma found Alfie's behaviour completely **un**acceptable.

The context of the sentence will help you work out which prefix or suffix is most suitable.

18) Billy made a delicious rubarb crumble — **rhubarb**
19) Lydia has an extensive nowledge of local history — **knowledge**
20) The pluming in the old house needed a complete overhaul — **plumbing**
21) The enormous cat riggled out from beneath the mauve sofa — **wriggled**
22) The marathon runner was very disiplined — he trained every day — **disciplined**

To spot silent letters, you can look out for particular letter combinations. For example, silent 'b' often comes after 'm', and silent 'k' or 'g' often come before 'n'.

23) We asessed the merits and pitfalls of the plan. — **assessed**
24) The artist had drawn fabulous ilustrations for the novel. — **illustrations**
25) The children colected petals from different flowers. — **collected**

Answers

26) We returned the uneeded cutlery to the cabinet. — **unneeded**
27) Some pigs have an apetite for truffles, so they rummage for them. — **appetite**

Double letters usually make a single sound, so it can be hard to spot when a letter is missing. Learn the most common words with double letters and make sure you can spell them correctly.

28) Tina has painted the walls an awful shade of beige.
The 'i' comes after 'e' in 'beige' because the 'ei' sound doesn't rhyme with 'bee'.
29) Grandad says he used to get up to all sorts of mischief at school.
The letter 'i' is before 'e' in 'mischief' because the 'ie' doesn't follow 'c' and its sound rhymes with 'bee'.
30) The lorries carried their heavy freight onto the ferry.
The 'i' comes after 'e' in 'freight' because the 'ei' sound doesn't rhyme with 'bee'.
31) Martin swaggered over with a conceited smile on his face.
The 'i' comes after 'e' because it follows 'c' and the 'ei' sound rhymes with 'bee'.
32) They heard a high-pitched shriek from the other room.
The letter 'i' is before 'e' in 'shriek' because the 'ie' sound rhymes with 'bee'.
33) The knight wielded the sword with great skill.
The letter 'i' is before 'e' in 'wielded' because the 'ie' sound rhymes with 'bee'.
34) Every Saturday, George went to the lib**r**ary to borrow a new book.
35) Annabel was extremely interested in archaeology.
36) I had to do the washing-up all week as a punishment.
37) Cara's office had to hire a new sec**re**tary after Kevin retired.
38) Attending the school fair was vol**un**tary, but everyone in Ola's class was going.

These vowels are all unstressed — they aren't clearly pronounced when the word is said out loud.

39) The soldiers stood defiently before the opposing battalion — **defiantly**
40) Mel requested that the publishers didn't altar any spellings — **alter**
41) We jogged along an indistinct footpath that ran paralel to the river — **parallel**
42) Jane was ingrossed in a lengthy biography — it had two volumes — **engrossed**
43) The professional jewel thieves scemed together before the heist — **schemed**
44) Milo found Cleo's allegations to be entirely implausable — **implausible**

Section Four — Writers' Techniques

Pages 64-65 — Alliteration and Onomatopoeia

1) a) neither
   b) onomatopoeia — the word 'banged' is onomatopoeic.
   c) alliteration — the 's' sound is repeated.
   d) neither
   e) neither
   f) onomatopoeia — the word 'clucked' is onomatopoeic.

Think about the sounds used at the start of each word rather than the letters — if the same sound repeats, it's alliteration. If there's a word which sounds like the noise it's describing, it's onomatopoeia.

Pages 66-68 — Imagery

1) a) personification — 'luck' is personified.
   b) simile — the phrase 'as ... as' shows that Fatima's clothes were like something else.
   c) personification — 'fear' is personified.
   d) simile — the phrase 'as ... as' shows that the packed classroom was like something else.
   e) metaphor — the sentence says that Gary's fingers 'were' something else.

If the sentence gives human qualities to anything other than a person, it's personification. If the sentence compares something to something else, it's an example of a simile. If the sentence says that something is something else then it's a metaphor.

Page 69 — Abbreviations

1) a) rhino
   b) email (or e-mail)
   c) flu

These are the abbreviations of the longer words.

2) a) dinosaur
   b) television
   c) laboratory

These are the full versions of the abbreviations.

3) a) initialism — 'CD' = compact disc.
   b) abbreviation — 'approx' = approximately.
   c) acronym — 'NASA' = National Aeronautical Space Agency.
   d) initialism — 'DVD' = digital versatile disc.
   e) initialism — 'BBC' = British Broadcasting Corporation.

Abbreviations are shortened versions of words. Initialisms take the first letter of every word in a phrase and pronounce each letter separately. Acronyms use the first letters of words in a phrase to make a new word.

Pages 70-71 — Irony and Rhetorical Questions

1)   **a)**, **c)** and **e)** no tick
    b) and **d)** tick

Situational irony is when the opposite happens to what the reader expects.

Pages 72-73 — Idioms, Clichés and Proverbs

1)   a) You're going to end up in trouble if you carry on like this.
    b) I put a lot of effort into my maths homework.
    c) It's time to give up.
    d) I wish the politician would stop avoiding the issue.
    e) My little brother is really annoying me.

Answers may vary for these questions, but make sure you have given the actual meaning for each sentence, rather than the literal meaning of the words.

Pages 74-75 — Synonyms and Antonyms

1)   a) hopeless
    b) threatening
    c) hurriedly

These are the synonyms for each of the words in bold.

2)   a) respectful
    b) despondent
    c) stimulating

These are the antonyms for each of the words in bold.

Pages 78-81 — Practice Questions

1) A loud <u>crackle</u> and a flash from the fire made Mr Cox jolt awake.
2) Their chatter subsided until only the <u>whistling wind</u> could be heard.
3) The full moon shone through the <u>cracks</u> in the <u>crumbling castle</u> walls.
4) With a <u>snap</u>, the ruler broke and flew across the room.
5) Joe was woken in the night by the <u>croaking</u> of the fat, green frogs.

Alliteration is the repetition of a sound at the beginning of nearby words. Onomatopoeia is when a word sounds like the noise it describes.

6) The fluffy clouds were **like cotton wool**.
7) The cat's eyes were **saucers**.
8) Dasha walked **as slowly as a sloth**.
9) The evil man's heart was **stone**.
10) Jamal climbed **as swiftly as a squirrel**.

The words in bold are suggestions. There are many other similes and metaphors you could have written.

11) **personification** — This contains personification because the old door 'let out a low groan' like a person.
12) **analogy** — This contains an analogy because 'finding a needle in a haystack' helps you to imagine how difficult it was.
13) **personification** — This contains personification because it makes it sound like the wind has the ability to bite.
14) **analogy** — This contains an analogy because 'There are statues less stiff than I am' helps you to imagine how badly the person dances.
15) **analogy** — This contains an analogy because 'boomed like bombs' helps you understand how loud the fireworks were.
16) **personification** — This contains personification because it makes it sound like the dust 'danced' like a person.

Personification is when an objects is described as having human features or behaving like a human. An analogy is a comparison that helps you understand or visualise something more clearly.

17) **initialism** — The letters in 'UFO' are pronounced separately. They stand for 'Unidentified Flying Object'.
18) **abbreviation** — 'maths' is a shortened form of the word 'mathematics'.
19) **acronym** — The letters in 'SCUBA' are pronounced as one word. They stand for 'Self-Contained Underwater Breathing Apparatus'.
20) **initialism** — The letters in 'VIP' are pronounced separately. They stand for 'Very Important Person'.
21) **abbreviation** — 'app' is a shortened form of the word 'application'.

Abbreviations are shortened versions of words. Initialisms use the first letters of words in a phrase and are said as letters. Acronyms use the first letters of words in a phrase to make a new word.

22) For the first time ever, Fazia left home early, only for the bus to be late. — **SI**
23) Manu ended his speech by saying, "Are uniforms really needed?" — **RQ**
24) After losing ten games, the manager was ecstatic with their performance. — **VI**
25) Mum said, "How many times do I have to tell you to set the table?" — **RQ**
26) "Having a cold is a lot of fun," Dad said, blowing his nose. — **VI**

Verbal irony is similar to sarcasm — this is when someone says the opposite of what they really mean. Situational irony is where the opposite thing happens to what the reader expects. A rhetorical question is a question that you're not expected to answer.

148

27) **cliché** — This is a common phrase often used to end fairy tales.
28) **idiom** — This phrase isn't meant literally — it is an idiom used to describe something as very easy.
29) **cliché** — This is a common phrase that means someone had a great time.
30) **idiom** — This phrase isn't meant literally. It means you think someone is joking or trying to trick you.
31) **idiom** — This phrase isn't referring to a literal board. It means that an idea wasn't successful and a new one needs to be thought up.
32) **cliché** — This is a common phrase meaning it's better for something to happen later than expected than for it not to happen at all.

Idioms are phrases that aren't meant literally — you just have to know what they mean. Clichés are phrases that are overused and have lost a lot of their impact.

33) E.g. **secretive** — Both 'mysterious' and 'secretive' can mean 'concealed'.
34) E.g. **gloom** — Both 'darkness' and 'gloom' can mean there is very little or no light.
35) E.g. **spectacular** — Both 'impressive' and 'spectacular' can be used to describe something that is awe-inspiring.
36) E.g. **functioning** — Both 'operating' and 'functioning' can mean 'working'.
37) E.g. **lifelike** — Both 'realistic' and 'lifelike' can mean something that looks real but isn't.

The words in bold are just some of the synonyms you could have chosen — you might have written something different.

38) E.g. **valuable** — 'worthless' means 'has value' while 'valuable' means 'has no value'.
39) E.g. **excess** — 'lack' means 'not enough' while 'excess' means 'more than enough'.
40) E.g. **unexceptional** — 'striking' means 'remarkable' while 'unexceptional' means 'unremarkable'.
41) E.g. **immaculate** — 'unkempt' means 'untidy' while 'immaculate' means 'very neat'.
42) E.g. **withering** — 'thriving' can mean 'growing' while 'withering' means 'wilting' or 'dying'.

The words in bold are just some of the antonyms you could have chosen — you might have written something different.

Section Five — Comprehension

Pages 82-83 — Reading the Text

1) a) Oti Debuski's stage name is Lavahead.
   b) The word "frontwoman" (line 7) can mean the same thing as "lead vocalist".
   c) Sonal works in a shop because in the passage it says that "she scanned through Oti's basket", which means that she was working on a till.
   d) Oti tells Sonal to shut her mouth because she was probably gaping at meeting a member of her favourite band.
   e) The evidence suggests that Sonal was feeling nervous because she stutters and Oti tells her to shut her mouth, probably because she is gaping. She also feels excited, because it was "the most exciting thing that had happened".

Try to mention all of the relevant information when you're writing an answer to a comprehension question.

Pages 88-89 — Practice Questions

1) **C**
   The passage says that the plague entered Eyam "inside a flea-infested box of cloth".
2) **C**
   The passage says that the villagers put money in "vinegar-filled grooves" to "kill infection on the coins' surfaces".
3) **B**
   Both of these words mean 'practical'.
4) **A**
   The author says that the villagers' decision was "heroic", which indicates that they find Eyam's choice impressive.
5) **B**
   White Hawk "was one of the most skilful and lucky hunters of his tribe", which means there must have been other hunters.
6) **D**
   White Hawk was a "skilful" hunter, which suggests he brings plenty of food back for his tribe.
7) **C**
   White Hawk expects to see a "path", "a crushed leaf", "a broken twig" or "the least trace of a footstep" as evidence that the ring was made by a person, but not flowers.
8) **D**
   White Hawk looks up because after hearing "the faint sounds of music in the air".

If you are not sure about an answer, go back to the information in the text to help you work it out.

Answers

Section Six — Writing

Pages 92-93 — Make a Plan

1) a) and b) Various answers possible.

Make sure your plan for a) includes points for the introduction, argument and conclusion of the essay. Make sure your plan for b) has points for a gripping beginning, at least one interesting event in the middle, and an ending that brings it to a conclusion.

Pages 94-95 — Write in Paragraphs

1) Following another run-in with Mr Ulrich, Gary had awaited his verdict nervously. // "Gary, this is the third time you've been sent to my office for lateness. You should know better," the headmaster said, "but I know the perfect punishment — Miss Levis needs help with the junior hockey team." // That was a month ago, and since then Gary had been coming to the threadbare pitch every week to help with coaching. It was a task he didn't enjoy — he disliked the children and he despised standing in the cold watching them play. // There was one child he truly hated: Brenda. She had been a nuisance from the start. She tied Gary's shoelaces together when he wasn't looking and took every opportunity to hit the ball at him. // "Stupid kids!" thought Gary, as it started to rain. "Stupid, rotten, silly kids!"

There should be a new paragraph when something changes.

Pages 96-98 — Make It Interesting

1) a) Various answers possible, e.g. 'nearby park', 'creaky swings', 'slippery slide', 'rickety roundabout'.

   b) Various answers possible, e.g. 'Old Mr Brown', 'stubborn cats', 'naughty cats'.

Make sure that the adjectives you added make sense in the sentence.

2) a) Various answers possible, e.g. 'consumed' or 'devoured', 'starving' or 'famished', 'disgusting' or 'horrible'.

   b) Various answers possible, e.g. 'dashed' or 'sprinted', 'gloomy' or 'murky', 'tripped' or 'slipped', 'bashed' or 'bruised'.

If you struggled to find a different word, try looking in a thesaurus.

Page 99 — Writing Practice

Writing Techniques

1) a) Various answers possible, e.g. 'It was a glorious day, so I ambled to the beach. First I built a massive sandcastle, then I gobbled a delicious ice cream.'

   b) Various answers possible, e.g. 'The enormous ogre was hideous. I felt so terrified that I crept behind a jagged rock and skulked there until he stomped away.'

   c) Various answers possible, e.g. '"Quick, give me the biggest fishing rod!" I yelled. I had seen a sudden movement in the murky depths. "Here you go," gasped Timmy, throwing me the rod. "It might not be sturdy enough — the Loch Ness monster is enormous. Here, take the reinforced net as well."'

You can add and replace adjectives, verbs and conjunctions to make the sentences more interesting. Try to use a variety of types and lengths of sentences to make your writing flow better.

2) a) Various answers possible, e.g. 'The sky was like freshly whipped cream.'

   b) Various answers possible, e.g. 'The meal was as hot as the surface of the sun.'

   c) Various answers possible, e.g. 'His hair was like the thatched roof of a tumbledown cottage.'

Try to make your similes appeal to the reader's senses, so they can clearly picture what you're describing.

Writing Fiction

1) a) Various answers possible, e.g. 'cruel', 'sneering', 'stooped', 'twisted', 'powerful'.

   b) Various answers possible, e.g. 'jolly', 'friendly', 'old', 'chubby', 'laughing'.

   c) Various answers possible, e.g. 'gruff', 'hairy', 'huge', 'gentle', 'strong'.

Picture your characters as clearly as you can. Think about how they look, sound and act.

2) a) Various answers possible, e.g. 'A dark, crooked tower near the top of a forbidding mountain.'

   b) Various answers possible, e.g. 'A cheerful, whitewashed cottage with a bright blue front door. The front garden is full of roses, and inside there is the warm smell of baking bread.'

   c) Various answers possible, e.g. 'A cosy den in a bright, sun-dappled forest. The floor is soft and mossy, and the space is filled with giant, pillowy armchairs and sturdy wooden furniture.'

Add as much detail to your descriptions as you can. Try to picture exactly where your character would live.

3) a) and b) Various answers possible.

Make sure your plans include points for the beginning, middle and end of your story.

4) Various answers possible.

Remember to use the techniques you've learnt to make your writing interesting. If you decide to answer b), check you have spelt the characters' names correctly, that you have copied the same style of writing, and have continued the story so it makes sense.

Writing Non-fiction

1) a) – c) Various answers possible.
Make sure your plans include points for the introduction, argument and conclusion of your essay.

2) Various answers possible.
Make sure you use the right sort of writing style. Question a) should be informative and balanced, and should be written in an informal style. Question b) should be persuasive, and should be written in a formal style. Question c) should include lots of interesting descriptions, and should be informal.

Pages 100-101 — Practice Questions

There are many possible answers to the questions on these pages. We've put some ideas below to help.

1) e.g. 'Faisa followed the dog **towards the old, run-down house.**'
2) e.g. 'I leapt over the gate **and sprinted past the bemused sheep.**'
3) e.g. 'The horse neighed, **alerting the robbers to our presence.**'
4) e.g. 'Everyone cheered **as our rickety go-kart finally crossed the finish line.**'
5) e.g. 'Drake drank his tea **in tiny sips, one finger delicately extended.**'
6) e.g. 'Elle opened the box, **biting her lip in anticipation.**'

You might have finished each sentence by adding more action or description. Make sure each completed sentence makes sense.

7) – 11) Various answers possible.
Make sure your plans have points for a gripping beginning, at least one interesting event in the middle, and an ending that brings the story to a conclusion. Each full story should follow its plan, but should be fleshed out with more detail and descriptions of events.

12) E.g. For: People talking can make it hard for others to concentrate.
Against: Discussing books can be interesting and educational.

13) E.g. For: Children can help their parents and learn useful skills.
Against: Children are already busy with schoolwork and hobbies.

14) E.g. For: It's a good way for students to experience other cultures.
Against: Overseas trips can be expensive for parents and schools.

These arguments are just exmaples — you might have written something different.

15) – 18) Various answers possible.
Make sure your plans include points for the introduction, argument and conclusion of the essay. Each full essay should follow its plan, but should be fleshed out with more detail, and should be written in a style that reflects its purpose.

Mixed Practice Tests

Pages 102-104 — Mixed Practice Test 1

1) **C**
In the poem, the ferns have "moisture dripping" from them, which means they must be damp.

2) **B**
In the poem, the cliffs are described as like "ramparts", which are 'the defensive walls of a castle'.

3) **D**
"rugged" is an adjective — it describes the noun "feet".

4) **C**
The third verse says that dust is "banished and forbidden" from the valleys.

5) **B**
The stream is "crooning" (singing) — this is personification because the stream is described as doing a human action.

6) **A**
The phrase "Now pouring down" relates to the water falling off the ledge to become a waterfall, so this verse doesn't mention rain.

7) **C**
It says that the fading light "softens ragged edges" which means that the low light makes the landscape look less harsh.

8) **B**
"placid" is closest in meaning to 'calm'.

9) **B**
'vibrent' should be 'vibrant' — the ending should be 'ant'.

10) **B**
'aray' should be 'array' — there should be a double 'r'.

11) **N**
There are no mistakes in this line.

12) **B**
'spectaculer' should be 'spectacular' — the unstressed vowel sound is spelt with an 'a'.

13) **A**
'wander' should be 'wonder'. These words are near homophones — 'wonder' is correct because it means 'an amazing thing'.

14) **A**
'at' is the only preposition that makes sense here.

Answers

15) **D**
'ran' is the correct past tense form of the verb 'to run'.

16) **E**
'due to' is the only option that makes sense here.

17) **A**
'hidden' is the correct past tense form of the verb 'to hide'.

18) **C**
'before' is the only option that makes sense here.

Pages 105-107 — Mixed Practice Test 2

1) **B**
In the passage, "abounded in" could be most accurately replaced by 'had plenty of'.

2) **B**
The passage says that "fears" stopped their mother and Elinor from joining them on the walk.

3) **D**
"driving" is closest in meaning to 'forceful'.

4) **C**
The passage says that the sudden "driving rain" left them "Chagrined", which suggests they didn't enjoy being in it.

5) **E**
"yards" is a common noun because it is the name for a measurement.

6) **D**
In the passage it says Marianne "had raised herself from the ground", so she was able to get up.

7) **C**
The passage says that Margaret was "involuntarily hurried along" as she ran down the hill, which suggests she couldn't control her speed.

8) **D**
Elinor and her mother are admiring the gentleman's appearance.

9) **N**
There are no mistakes in this line.

10) **D**
'dutifly' should be 'dutifully' — the root word is 'dutiful'.

11) **B**
'forege' should be 'forage' — the ending should be 'age'.

12) **D**
'predaters' should be 'predators' — the unstressed vowel sound is spelt with an 'o'.

13) **D**
'independense' should be 'independence' — the ending should be 'ence'.

14) **D**
'friends' should be 'friend's' — the apostrophe shows that the phrase book belongs to the friend.

15) **D**
There should be a comma after 'cold' to separate the fronted adverbial from the rest of the sentence.

16) **A**
The semi-colon after 'packed' should be a colon, because it is introducing a list.

17) **B**
'winter-clothes' should be 'winter clothes' — the hyphen isn't needed.

18) **N**
There are no mistakes in this line.

Pages 108-110 — Mixed Practice Test 3

1) **C**
The passage says Venice is known as a 'floating city' because "Wooden stilts were used as the foundations for buildings".

2) **A**
The word which best describes Venice is 'bustling' because tourists "flock" to the city.

3) **E**
"world-renowned" means 'recognised all over the world'.

4) **A**
"international" is an adjective because it describes the noun "centre".

5) **B**
Although the passage mentions that visitors may "take a trip" in a gondola, there is no mention of learning how to punt.

6) **C**
"elaborate" means the same as 'detailed'.

7) **D**
"intensified" is closest in meaning to 'heightened' — both words mean 'increased'.

8) **B**
The passage says that "Every year floodwaters submerge the streets", and that by 2100 Venice could be "uninhabitable".

9) **B**
The semi-colon after 'please' should be a colon, because it is introducing a list.

10) **B**
'potter' should have a capital letter because it is a proper noun.

11) **B**
The comma should come inside the inverted commas at the end of the speech.

12) **N**
There are no mistakes in this line.

13) **D**
'it's' should be 'its' — there shouldn't be an apostrophe because 'its' shows possession in this sentence.

Answers

14) **A**
'for' is correct because it completes the phrase 'cared for'.

15) **E**
'Despite' is the only option that makes sense here.

16) **C**
'allow' is the only option that makes sense here.

17) **B**
'prior' is correct because it completes the phrase 'prior to'.

18) **A**
'can' is the only option that makes sense here.

Pages 111-113 — Mixed Practice Test 4

1) **C**
"fateful" is closest in meaning to 'significant'.

2) **B**
The passage says it will be "more than eighteen years" before the moon next has the right "conditions".

3) **B**
"charged with the duty" means the same as 'given the job' in this context.

4) **D**
The phrases "dry eyes" and "one ancient tear" suggest that Maston doesn't cry very often, which implies that he doesn't often show emotion.

5) **D**
The silence is described as "terrible" which suggests that the spectators feel tense.

6) **A**
"wanted scarce forty seconds" means that it is forty seconds until the moment of departure.

7) **C**
"departure" is a common noun because it's the name of an action. It's also an abstract noun because you can't see or touch it — abstract nouns are a type of common noun.

8) **A**
The passage says that the travellers took their place in the projectile when "Ten o'clock struck!"

9) **A**
'unnusual' should be 'unusual' — the prefix is 'un'.

10) **N**
There are no mistakes in this line.

11) **D**
'practiced' should be 'practised' — 'practised' should be spelt with an 's' because it's a verb.

12) **C**
'posess' should be 'possess' — there is a double 's' in the middle of the word.

13) **B**
'incredibley' should be 'incredibly' — the 'e' at the end of 'incredible' is removed when the 'ly' ending is added.

14) **B**
'almost' is the only option that makes sense here.

15) **B**
'were' is the correct past tense form of the verb 'to be'.

16) **E**
'only' is the only option that makes sense here.

17) **B**
'because' is the only option that makes sense here.

18) **D**
'knew' is the correct past tense form of the verb 'to know'.

Practice Papers

Pages 114-125 — Practice Paper 1

1) **D**
In the passage, the foxes are "playing together", "leaping" and "grappling", which suggests they are full of energy.

2) **B**
"met their mood" means 'suited how they felt', so playing is all they feel like doing.

3) **C**
The foxes are "just about to grapple" when they notice the trail and immediately stop — this shows that they take the potential danger seriously.

4) **E**
Once the foxes know the trail isn't fresh, they examine it in a "wondering" way which shows they are curious.

5) **A**
They initially think it is "a monster" — they don't realise it's a "man" until later in the text.

6) **C**
"dispenser of fire and noise and death" refers to Jabe Smith shooting and killing animals in the forest, as firing a gun produces a flash of light and a loud noise. Jabe Smith is also described as a 'trapper' later in the text, which confirms that he kills wild animals.

7) **D**
Red Fox doesn't understand why Jabe Smith wears snow-shoes because "men are mysterious", but he is happy to "let the question go at that" which shows he isn't interested in finding out more about them.

8) **E**
The path leads to a place that is a "section of the she-fox's range", which means she has been there before.

9) **C**
The word "prize" shows that the chicken head is attractive to Red Fox and suggests it's something he'd be excited about eating.

10) **A**
The she-fox pushing Red Fox makes him realise "the presence of an unknown peril", so she is warning him about danger.

11) **C**
The fact that no tracks can be seen is ominous because it suggests that someone has hidden them to lure the foxes to the chicken head, which could be dangerous for the foxes.

12) **B**
The Red Fox didn't know that there was something buried under the snow, but the she-fox knew there was something "terribly dangerous" there.

13) **C**
The she-fox "dared not disturb" the snow in the middle of the trap, which shows that she knows they need to be very careful.

14) **E**
The she-fox "flatly discouraged" Red Fox from examining the trap.

15) **C**
The she-fox teaches him that "unexpected blessings, like the chicken head" were likely to "indicate at least one trap" nearby.

16) **A**
They leave the trap uncovered so that "no other of the forest dwellers might be betrayed by it", which means they don't want any other animals to step into the trap as Red Fox nearly did.

17) **B**
They are looking for "more treasons" planted by Jabe Smith.

18) **C**
They don't know what made the strange sound they hear, so they move cautiously, not wanting to reveal themselves, in case it's something dangerous.

19) **D**
"stupendous" is closest in meaning to 'astonishingly large' — the foxes are shocked by how big the feet that made the tracks seem to be.

20) **E**
"obtained" could most accurately be replaced by 'gained' — the words both mean 'to get something'.

21) **C**
"timidity" could most accurately be replaced by 'fear' here — the she-fox is being extremely careful because she's afraid of what lies beneath the snow.

22) **B**
"daunting" is closest in meaning to 'intimidating' — both words can mean 'frightening'.

23) **B**
"swish" and "crackle" are both examples of onomatopoeia, because they sound like the noise they describe.

24) **D**
These words are all verbs — they tell you what actions are being done.

25) **A**
"wariness" is a common noun because it's the name of a feeling. It's also an abstract noun because you can't see or touch it — abstract nouns are a type of common noun.

26) **B**
The phrase contains alliteration as "trapper's" and "trail" both begin with the letter 't'.

27) **N**
There are no mistakes in this line.

28) **A**
'luxurius' should be 'luxurious'.

29) **B**
'custommers' should be 'customers'.

30) **B**
'sumtuous' should be 'sumptuous'.

31) **A**
'legendery' should be 'legendary'.

32) **D**
'wierd' should be 'weird' — the word is an exception to the 'i' before 'e' rule.

33) **B**
'vegetarien' should be 'vegetarian'.

34) **C**
'strait' should be 'straight'. These words are homophones — they sound the same but are spelt differently.

35) **B**
'its' should be 'it's' — it is a contraction of 'it has', so you need an apostrophe to indicate the missing letters.

36) **A**
There should be a dash (—) or a colon (:) between 'it' and 'she's'.

37) **N**
There are no mistakes in this line.

38) **A**
'dr' should be 'Dr'.

39) **D**
There shouldn't be a comma after 'footsteps' — 'Approaching footsteps' isn't a fronted adverbial or a subordinate clause.

40) **D**
'friend's' should be 'friends'' — the apostrophe comes after the 's' because it is showing that the faces belong to more than one friend.

Answers

41) **B**

There should be inverted commas after 'you!' to mark the end of Granny's direct speech.

42) **D**

The full stop after 'costume' should be a question mark.

43) **D**

'will' is the only option that makes sense here.

44) **A**

'Their' is the correct spelling of the possessive determiner. In this case it is referring to the competitors.

45) **A**

'held' is the correct past tense form of the verb 'to hold'.

46) **C**

'Whichever' is the only option that makes sense here.

47) **B**

'were' is the only option that makes sense here.

48) **D**

'but' is the only conjunction that makes sense here.

49) **A**

'Those' is the correct pronoun to replace 'people' as the subject of the sentence.

50) **C**

'before' is the only conjunction that makes sense here — the event is yet to happen.

Pages 126-137 — Practice Paper 2

1) **C**

The narrator was "intending" to go to the Amazon, but he ends up going to California and the Yosemite Valley instead.

2) **E**

The narrator says that he was "unable to find a ship bound for South America", which leads to him changing his plans.

3) **B**

"drenched" has a similar meaning to "flooded", which suggests that there is lots of sunshine in the valley and therefore it would be very bright.

4) **D**

The narrator says that the hills look "painted" with flowers, which suggests that they're colourful.

5) **D**

When the narrator is in the Santa Clara Valley, he says that the "Yosemite Valley lay to the east", which means that the Santa Clara Valley is to the west of the Yosemite Valley.

6) **A**

The narrator describes the rocks as being the size of mountains, but he doesn't say they're all part of the same mountain.

7) **E**

The narrator has been describing how impressive Yosemite is, so he means that man-made temples are less impressive in comparison with Yosemite.

8) **D**

"animation" has a similar meaning to 'liveliness', so the narrator is saying that the insects and birds help to create a lively atmosphere.

9) **B**

"cultivation" has a similar meaning to 'farming'.

10) **A**

"choicest" is closest in meaning to 'prime' — the narrator is saying that nature has collected her best treasures together in Yosemite.

11) **B**

"progress" is a noun because it is the name of a concept. It's also an abstract noun because you can't see or touch it — abstract nouns are a type of common noun.

12) **E**

"alone" is an adverb here because it describes how the narrator travelled.

13) **C**

This is personification because the rocks are described as having "thoughtful attitudes", which makes them seem human.

14) **E**

Line 1 says that the tulip "had offered to hold" the butterfly, which shows that it is 'welcoming'.

15) **C**

"fancy" means 'imagination' and "range" means 'move about freely', so the poet is saying that the butterfly's imagination is free to wander.

16) **D**

"despise" means 'hate' and "could but" is a shorter way of saying 'could not help but', which suggests that the butterfly can't avoid doing it.

17) **A**

The poet says that the bees have come into the garden "for their winter supplies", which shows that they're collecting food for winter.

18) **E**

The butterfly calls the bees "unworthy" and "a rabble too low", which suggests he thinks that they aren't important enough to come near him.

19) **C**

The word "fenced" suggests that the bees have encircled the butterfly.

20) **E**

The poet describes the hum of the bees as "a cannon-peal", which is the sound of a cannon firing.

Answers

21) **C**
Line 38 says that "His head ached — his throne reeled and fell", which shows that the butterfly feels ill and he falls to the ground.

22) **D**
"unworthy" is an adjective because it describes the bees (in the butterfly's opinion).

23) **B**
This is a simile because it is describing something as being like something else.

24) **D**
"diligent" is closest in meaning to 'conscientious' — they both refer to doing something thoroughly.

25) **E**
"ire" is closest in meaning to 'fury' — both words mean 'anger'.

26) **B**
"reeled" could most accurately be replaced by 'swayed' — both words mean 'move unsteadily'.

27) **B**
'conservatry' should be 'conservatory' — there is an unstressed 'o'.

28) **B**
'layed' should be 'laid' — the past tense of 'lay' is 'laid'.

29) **D**
'desserted' should be 'deserted' — the root word is 'desert'.

30) **N**
There are no mistakes in this line.

31) **C**
'climed' should be 'climbed' — the root word is 'climb', which contains a silent 'b'.

32) **C**
'gooses' should be 'geese' — the plural of 'goose' is 'geese'.

33) **D**
'metalic' should be 'metallic' — the word is spelt with a double 'l'.

34) **A**
'siezed' should be 'seized' — the word is an exception to the 'i' before 'e' rule.

35) **B**
There shouldn't be a comma after 'peace' — commas are only needed in lists with three or more items.

36) **D**
'sheds' should begin with a capital letter because it is part of the name of a company.

37) **B**
There should be a hyphen between 'world' and 'leading' to make the meaning clearer.

38) **A**
There shouldn't be an apostrophe in 'customer's' — this is a plural not a possessive noun.

39) **C**
There shouldn't be a colon after 'life's' because the bit before the colon doesn't make sense on its own.

40) **N**
There are no mistakes in this line.

41) **B**
'Heres' needs an apostrophe because it is a contraction of 'Here is'.

42) **D**
The exclamation mark should be inside the inverted commas.

43) **C**
'amazed' is correct because it completes the phrase 'were amazed by'.

44) **D**
'Expecting' is the only option that makes sense here.

45) **B**
'instead' is the correct option because it's the only adverb that helps to show what happened in place of the normal tour.

46) **B**
'about' is the only option that makes sense here as the tour guide is giving the performance to the visitors (not the past residents).

47) **A**
'No one' is the only pronoun that makes sense here.

48) **C**
'to deviate' is the only option that fits with 'chose yesterday'.

49) **E**
'has been' is correct because it completes the phrase 'has been rumoured'.

50) **D**
'Whatever' is the correct option because it's used when referring to an unknown thing (rather than a person or place).

Index

A
abbreviations 69
acronyms 69
active verbs 7
adjectives , 10, 11
adverbials 15, 33
adverbs 10, 11
alliteration 64, 65
analogies 67
antonyms 74, 75
apostrophes 36, 37

B
brackets 34

C
capital letters 30-32
clauses 14-16, 33, 40
clichés 72
colons 40, 41
commas 33, 34, 38
comparatives 10
comparisons 90, 97
complex sentences 14, 17
compound sentences 15, 17
comprehension 23-25, 82-87
conjunctions 14, 15, 18, 19
consonants 48

D
dashes 34
descriptive writing 91
determiners 12, 13
double letters 54, 55

E
ellipses 31
ending sentences 30-32
exaggeration 97
exclamation marks 30, 32, 38

F
figurative language 66
formal writing 20
full stops 30, 31, 38

G
grammar 4-25, 85

H
homographs 50
homophones 50, 51
hyphens 36

I
'i before e' rule 56, 57
idioms 72, 73
imagery 66-68
indirect speech 38
informative writing 91
initialisms 69
inverted commas 38, 39
irony 70, 71

L
letters 91
literal language 66

M
main clauses 14, 15, 34, 40
metaphors 67
modal verbs 8
Multiple Choice Questions 22, 23, 42, 58, 76, 86

N
noun phrases 16
nouns 4-6

O
onomatopoeia 64

P
paragraphs 94, 95
passive verbs 7
personification 67, 68
persuasive writing 91
planning 92, 93
plurals 48, 49
prefixes 36, 52, 53, 74
preposition phrases 16
prepositions 10, 16
pronouns 5, 6
proverbs 72
punctuation 30-43
puns 50

Q
question marks 31, 38

R
rhetorical questions 70

S
semicolons 40, 41
sentences 14, 15, 30, 17, 31
silent letters 54, 55
similes 66
spelling 48-59
spider diagrams 93
Standard Answer Questions 24, 25, 43, 59, 77, 87
Standard English 20
starting sentences 30
subject 7
subjunctive 20
subordinate clauses 14, 18, 33
suffixes 52, 53, 74
superlatives 10
synonyms 74, 75

T
tenses 7, 9

U
unstressed vowels 56

V
verbs 7-9, 14
vocabulary 90
vowels 48

W
writers' techniques 64-77
writing questions 90-98
    fiction 90, 92
    non-fiction 91, 92